WITHOUT YOUR JOB TITLE, WHO ARE YOU?

Soumana Ammar

PASSIONPRENEUR®
PUBLISHING

WITHOUT YOUR JOB TITLE, WHO ARE YOU?

Soumana Ammar

PASSIONPRENEUR® PUBLISHING

Without Your Job Title, Who Are You?
Copyright © 2023 Soumana Ammar
First published in 2023

Print: 978-1-76124-125-3
E-book: 978-1-76124-126-0

Because of the dynamic nature of the Internet, any web addresses or links contained in this book may have changed since publication and may no longer be valid. The information in this book is based on the author's experiences and opinions. The views expressed in this book are solely those of the author and do not necessarily reflect the views of the publisher; the publisher hereby disclaims any responsibility for them.

The author of this book does not dispense any form of medical, legal, financial, or technical advice either directly or indirectly. The intent of the author is solely to provide information of a general nature to help you in your quest for personal development and growth. In the event you use any of the information in this book, the author and the publisher assume no responsibility for your actions. If any form of expert assistance is required, the services of a competent professional should be sought.

Publishing information
Publishing and design facilitated by
Passionpreneur Publishing,
A division of Passionpreneur Organization Pty Ltd,
ABN: 48640637529

Melbourne, VIC | Australia
www.PassionpreneurPublishing.com

To Mom, who encouraged me to fly toward my dreams.

TABLE OF CONTENTS

ACKNOWLEDGEMENTS

Thanks to my family, my mom, my brother Sari and my sisters Sahar and Sareen for always embracing me with love and care. You motivate me, appreciate me, love me and nurture me. You always believed in me and held my hand. I love you all so very much.

Thanks to my nephews and nieces who showed me the meaning of selfless love, for giving me some of the most precious life lessons and for filling my life with beautiful emotions. You are my heroes. You make me proud of being an aunt. I love you.

Thank you, Maggie Z. Al Mandeel, for the generosity and inspiration. You encourage me to dream.

Thanks to my cousins for being the best extended family anyone can ever have. You have shown a profound belief in my work. I love you.

Thank you, Katrina S. Ammar, for making me feel like the sister you never had and cheering me up.

A special thank you to you, Lionella Todirean for having been a mirror through the beginning of my journey and you continue to be. I appreciate you. You never hesitated to show up for me. You always keep reminding me of my worth and fuelling my passion for pursuing my dreams.

To all my teachers along the way: Ian Taylor, Diana Mruk, Akmo Bolotbek kyzy and everyone who has crossed my path to teach me valuable lessons that I will cherish for life, I am grateful.

To all my friends who have been my cheerleaders, thank you. I have missed many fun times with you while writing this book, but you were always cheering from far or near. I love each and every one of you. You have shown a profound belief in my work. Thank you!

Thank you, Kelly Bone, for being a role model, a friend, and a soul-sister. You have been cheering me up for more than 21 years and I am grateful for you. You are a gift to this world.

Thank you, Sophia Bakkal, for the kindness and warmth of true friendship for all the years that I have known you and for being the bubbly beautiful soul. I carry this in my heart forever and I will always remember you. I know you will be smiling at me from up above.

Thank you, Nisrine Karazi, for the courage and the meaning of pursuing our dreams.

Thank you, Marianna Rosset, for the guidance and pushing me towards this dream in your own unique way. Your energy motivates me towards abundance.

Thank you, Sophie Tamer, for the appreciation and recognition throughout all the years.

Thank you CD Kotze for the encouragement and the partnership in growing people.

Thank you, Mariana Missakian, for the individuality and your unique nature.

Thank you, Lorraine Taylor, for the invaluable insights and encouragement.

Thank you, Lucile Falguieres, for the friendship, creativity and fun times during our photography projects.

Thank you, Karen Joyce, for always being there and for the countless memories.

Thank you, Karim El Horr for the support and encouragement, Olimpia Grassi for the adventures and the generosity, Abier Wasouf for the motivation and love, Rania Braiteh for your friendship and presence, Zahirah Marty for the motivation, Nada Fatayry for the infectious enthusiasm and positivity, Nadine Azar for the fun memories and encouragement, Linda Saab for the beautiful shared experiences and deep discussions, Nisrine Azar for the light-heartedness and transparency, Tagreeed Saab for always being my cheerleader, Samar Abdallah for the abundant friendship, Maya Salameh for the lovely times and lifelong dances, Darine Badreddine for the unwavering optimism and support, Rania Keedy for the uplifting comments at every interaction, Laura Ciciulla for the fun times and creative experiences, Carla Boustany for all the motivation and belief you reflect, Maya Taher for the motivation and respecting the dedication I poured into this book, Nimati Emam for your inspiration and spontaneous nature.

Thank you, Shraddha Carlin, for your encouragement and unconditional friendship, Minal Patel for contagious passion for creativity, Stephanie Zehetner for your enthusiasm and adventures.

Thank you Shari Lineberger for your motivation and pioneering nature.

Thank you Hady Safa for you unwavering support and being a tremendous source of motivation.

To my colleagues and team members who have helped me grow to the leader I aspired to become, thank you. You have trusted me, and I am thankful for that.

To the leaders who have trusted me throughout the years, thank you for the encouragement, guidance and appreciation.

To team members who stood by me like family and supported me through the writing process. Thank you, Olga Nianchuk, Jen Soque and Alem Hailu.

Thank you, Carmen and Eduardo, for being my family in Malaga. I know I will always have a home there. Muchas Gracias!

Thank you, Clarence Seedorf, for the valuable insightful discussions and the wisdom you shared to focus on our own path.

I gratefully acknowledge the advice and support of Ken Walls who helped me share my story and offered me invaluable advice.

Thanks to all my classmates who have embraced me with enthusiasm and support. Special thank you Daria Smith for your belief in my inspiration, Faeez Rajah for your presence and nurturing, Talal Ratrout for your trust and cheering, Nino Kogua for the immediate friendship, and Sima Qafiti for the ongoing acknowledgment.

Thanks to the DO!BrandYOU Community for their continuous support. We have grown together and you showed me the true meaning of embracing vulnerability.

Thank you Jeanette Tamer for translating my words into beautiful illustrations.

And I would like to share my sincere gratitude to the Passionpreneur team for helping share my story to the world. Your creative vision has helped me transform this book into an engaging experience.

Above all, my heart is filled with gratitude to life with all its adventures. Gratitude is where life gives life to life.

INTRODUCTION

Without your job title, who are you? When asked, this question can cause people to feel extremely vulnerable. Thinking about who you are without your title is like stepping out from behind a mask. We get conditioned throughout the years that titles represent our identity. Whilst the definition of success is very subjective, the drive towards a title becomes the main focus. Whilst career titles represent a huge part of many of our lives, we can add to that and build a more balanced identity in line with our values.

During my personal journey of self-exploration, I was searching for a deeper understanding that guided me to identify my purpose without being impacted by any label.

Once I stepped into my true identity, I started living an authentic life, stepping into the human being and the leader I aspired to be.

If it resonates with you, always aim to be yourself and not follow what you believe to be considered successful, just because of someone else's journey.

This book is for you to explore, reflect on, and enjoy. To get the best out of this book, develop a desire to know if some of the stories and questions resonate with you. Be open to seeing how you can apply some of the suggestions and tools during the journey.

CHAPTER 1

BREAKDOWN OR BREAKTHROUGH

WHAT HAPPENS WHEN LIFE CALLS YOU TO LOOK INSIDE?

In this story, I share my own journey of self-development and how I had to look into identifying my own values and my true purpose in life. This may sound, to some, like an easy thing to face. It may sound cliché to explore this, especially considering the fact that there are a lot of stories around offering a variety of tools and ways of looking at identifying your own values and your purpose. However, my story is personal. It is about a journey that I had to encounter on my own self-development, which had led me to believe that we are not able to reach the core of our own purpose except through our self-journey on the path of personal development.

Self-development is directly associated with self-awareness.

SELF-DEVELOPMENT
is directly associated with
SELF-AWARENESS.

My journey started when Covid hit. However, rewind to a time before the pandemic when I had appointed a life coach, my dearest Lionella, who was going to help me look at various aspects of my life, identify different perspectives and work with accountability towards some personal goals that I wanted to achieve. That was not business coaching related but more life-style related. The coaching was going well. We went into deep conversations on what had been stopping me from pursuing certain dreams, relooking at future plans, analysing upcoming emotions, and seeing a change of perspective with regards to what I was going through. I also participated in group medi-tation challenges that were kind of new to me. In my head, I was telling myself: "This is going to be the best year ever. You are putting all the effort and you are ticking off the winning formula." During our sessions, Lionella suggested that, since I have the qualities of a coach, it would be a great opportunity for me to equip myself with that skill set through an extension of my existing knowledge.

Of course, during the pandemic, I was observing the effect of this in society. I am looking around and there is something that is not clear, a high level of uncertainty. Being the posi-tive person that I am and having always been identified as an optimist, I displayed resilience and acceptance of what was going on.

I have spoken to Lionella about it, and that was kind of the best opportunity to take some coaching courses that could shift my mind into a different perspective and expand my knowledge. I always loved to work on people development. With my love of tango dancing and my commitment to personal growth, I wrote an article and posted it on LinkedIn. The article was called "It's Not Covid-19, It's Pivot-2020." In dance, a pivot turn (or simply a pivot) is a type of dance turn in which the performer's torso rotates around its vertical axis while remaining stationary.

PIVOT 2020

Here is my article and my emotions expressed at that point in time.

3

"Navigating the uncertainty we are all facing hasn't been the easiest of tasks for everyone. Doubt has taken over, fear is creeping, the future is unclear. Overthinking is becoming the new way of thinking. It is important to know that you are not alone. Millions of people around the world are like you. They need to know how to navigate during this time.

The current situation is a sign that something greater must happen. We should avoid ignorance in this age of information. We need to remember that this time is for us to step into creativity and creation. It's time for us to study, learn, change, execute, practice, and stand in the face of challenges with a greater level of mind.

We need to remember that we have the choice. We have the choice to sit and watch and feel sorry for ourselves. We can surrender to a victim mentality. We can surrender to fear and worry. We will be destined to be on the same path. It has been said that if we continue thinking the same thoughts, we will only exercise the same behaviours, and we will also have more of the emotions of fear and worry.

We also have the choice to be self-empowered, the knowledge of the self. We have the choice to pivot our own way. We have the choice to determine where we want to focus. We can tell ourselves: 'I will not allow myself to be defined by these thoughts and this path. These situations will not shape my future, I will PIVOT. I will rehearse my future, I will PIVOT.

- I will PIVOT, I will take a step back and look inside my heart and choose the perspective I want to see in the future with.
- I will PIVOT. I will open my mind to new ideas.

- I will PIVOT. I will list a handful of people who could be the perfect fit to be the right role model for me and I will learn from them.
- I will PIVOT. I will write down the emotions I feel and the actions I can take, instead of engaging these negative emotions.
- I will PIVOT. I will take actions that are positively impacting my physical and mental health.
- I will PIVOT. I will learn to forget those who hurt me and move through my life with a clean heart.
- I will PIVOT. I will plan my behaviours daily, reflecting my coherence with my heart and mind.
- I will PIVOT. I will keep cultivating elevated emotions of gratitude, love, appreciation, joy, enthusiasm, trust, compassion and appreciation.
- I will PIVOT. I will practice and write five things that I'm grateful for every morning or every evening.
- I will PIVOT. I will meditate daily. I will pivot, I will learn the hobby I always wanted to learn.
- I will PIVOT. I will say no to anything that doesn't vibrate with my personal values.
- I will PIVOT. I will create a list of random actions of kindness and perform some of them.
- I will PIVOT. I will identify what raises my energy to elevated emotions and create new habits.
- I will PIVOT. I will lead my life with consciousness and awareness. I am my inner leader.
- I will PIVOT. I will look at my challenges as something positive, an opportunity to build solutions and pivot.

- I will PIVOT. I will be consistent in the actions that are moving me to my future self. I will master my actions.
- I will PIVOT. I will unleash my inner leader.

I am on the way to being the best version of myself. I am the honour of my life. I took the choice: I will prime my brain into the future. I choose to PIVOT.'"

Of course, with all this positive energy and with all this pivoting that I wanted to put out there into the world, everybody thought, "Oh wow, that's a great article. I love your energy." My intention was to try to put this vision into action. Because of all the learning that I've been doing and all the books that I've been reading throughout the years, I have decided that this is the time for me to look at everything only from a positive mindset.

However, I did not consciously know that this was going to be the struggle, the breakdown that I would go through. Although I have been positive throughout the years, trying to study coaching and trying to understand what coaching means whilst putting my vision into action, I faced a crash of identity. When you are being coached, much "stuff" comes up; I call them "stuff" because this could refer to all the baggage of ideas that we carry with us throughout our years.

The struggle was that I started to explore more myself and had been unable to step out from the mask of being such an expert in an industry in which I am very comfortable. That industry is hospitality, to speak more also about my own beliefs and definition of success.

Getting more clarity on self-leadership, I had no clue about why I felt what I'd been feeling. I saw actions and behaviours around me that might have looked normal before but now seemed unacceptable in my opinion. I couldn't put my finger on it. "Why did I identify myself with certain behaviours that have permeated through the years and that maybe I picked up from other people?" The struggle was real.

A CRISIS OF THE SELF

This has been a real identity crisis. We might also refer to it as a crisis of "your self." Some call it a mid-life crisis. I don't know: terminology abounds. But what I can reassure you is that a breakdown brought on by identifying your-self to a certain set of beliefs and that causes you to look at your purpose without being connected to a company or a title or anything that defines you isn't the easiest of the of paths; however, it is definitely the most worth it. Everybody should go through their own unique self-journey in personal development in order for them to be able to lean on their strengths and on what makes them who they truly are, not what society or the environment has shaped them to be. The I PIVOT article was brought to life and was put into action, but little did I know that it would be my breakdown to breakthrough.

When I was going through my coaching courses, some questions started to come to mind:

- What if I am not successful?
- Why have I been playing "small" throughout the years?
- What am I: a hotel leader or a coach?
- What does authentic leadership mean?
- What defines our success?
- What differentiates good leaders from bosses?
- Why do company values matter and how do they differ from our own values?

Above all, the question that came coming up was:
- "What will people think?"

During the pandemic, everybody was putting information out into the market; however, I was not somebody who was actively speaking about my own opinions or was out there being interviewed or asked questions relating to personal development. I have practiced mentoring many team members all throughout my career. Coaching and mentoring others has been a core activity in every role I have taken. However, now it was time to speak about it.

One of the action steps (set to me by my coach) was to start sharing my own opinion on different platforms. I chose to use LinkedIn. After a few posts, I was contacted by a dear ex-colleague of mine, CD, who used to be in the hospitality industry, a big advocate of coaching and personal development, but now has his own coaching business. He asked me if I would be interested in running a Clubhouse room for hospitality industry people from all around the world to support them during these uncertain times. I embraced my vulnerability during that period. I was going through a self-journey myself but I did accept, to be there as my true self, and my true self was my authentic self.

This was the time where I felt the huge amount of vulnerability. This word "vulnerability" was new to me. I knew what it meant but I never knew how it felt until then. I only used to listen to people who had shown a lot of resilience, a lot of hard work, but I didn't yet know that there needed to be a dropping of the social mask. I reached a conclusion that we only heal ourselves by helping others. The sessions we did on Club House were rewarding. We chose topics that supported a lot of people and it was our way of giving back to the community. Throughout the years, I have learnt that two of the most valuable things you can give to anyone is your time and your energy. Here we were, giving both our time and energy for the sake of a greater good.

We only *heal* ourselves
BY HELPING OTHERS.

I started to be active in what I was learning, but in my mind I had many questions. I know who I am in my industry; but who am I, if not the person with that very title in my industry? This can apply to anybody, in any industry. I admire anyone in the hospitality industry. It's the industry of people, and I love people. But who am I without that? Today, if I wasn't part of that industry, and if I had been one of those people to lose a job during moments of mass layoffs and restructurings, what would I identify myself as?

With the "Who am I?" question, there was also a "What do I represent?" Why do I find it very hard to label myself as a coach although I have been doing it for my entire life? Was it me or my ego involved? I've been leading people all my life. That's what I know. I believe that I have been able to impact a number of them to take better decisions, either personally or professionally. I've always been an advocate of mentoring, but why do I find it so hard now to start to learn something from scratch and explore my inner self more deeply? It takes courage and acceptance. I needed to be vulnerable and true to myself in order to answer all these questions.

YEAR OF VULNERABILITY

That year was my "year of vulnerability" because I was looking at myself in the mirror, straight to the depths of my core, and saying, "Who are you? What are your values? What is your purpose? What really makes you tick?" This book is a reflection on my journey, to showcase the importance of being authentic, and the power we have when we come out of our shell and shed the notion that we are nothing but a title. Before we are a title in a company or in anything that we are doing, we are human beings. Whether you are an artist or an author, or any other role you perform, you're *self-leading*. Your creativity must be guided by you. You must drive it. You are a leader in your own life regardless of whatever title you carry. Your life is being led by you. You are aware that by leading your life, you have an impact on your subsequent actions. Your *personal brand* is you!

It is true that the choices you make can affect how your life turns out. Additionally, you must base your choices on a specific set of principles, and they must make sense. Perhaps you may have experienced situations in which you made a decision and felt awful about it, only to later learn that your decision was probably not aligned with some of your values. However, most people don't have this realisation and this insight is not widely held.

Hence I started this journey, which we'll talk about more in the next few chapters. Thousands of engagements on LinkedIn and other platforms were beginning to emerge as a result of me opining my thoughts on leadership, development, personal development, and authenticity. I had speeches to give. Others were getting in touch with me to talk about this journey I had taken. I had some public speaking engagements in the field of leadership and development as well as the personal journey of self-development. This was not a question of an expert journey in a specific industry. It was merely a question of a journey in people development. I understood that people wanted to hear what I had to say, and they *needed* to hear it. This was applicable to anyone in *any* industry. I had seen that many people were stuck in the deep grooves of inauthentic living and a lack of purpose. I was emerging as an authority in this self-development field.

UN-LABELLING AND RE-LABELLING

My struggle was that I was labelled as a female leader in the hospitality industry for more than twenty years, which is an amazing and proud accomplishment of mine, and I would not want that changed in any way. However, I needed to un-label and relabel. I needed to relabel myself as an advocate of people development. My goal was to research the school of thinking that would be most beneficial to me, aside from the skills I learned from the many books I had read. I therefore had the opportunity to hone my coaching skills with select clients.

I had a client who was about to drop a business. They had quite a new business that has recently started. They came to me for coaching and support. During my first meeting with that amazing and very successful company leader, I refused to do the business coaching before we did the personal coaching. A thought then entered my mind. If you change the person, the business will be affected because it's possible that some of the decisions they're making are motivated by internal conflicts, personal struggles or other issues.

I always dreamt of writing a book. Here I am being identified as an author, and I have quite the strength and the confidence to design my life because what I care about is to embrace and identify my divine self. Throughout a few of the coaching sessions I was leading, I was helping aspiring leaders and entrepreneurs who were going through a journey of self-awareness. The outcome was that I was impacting authentic human leadership in my own way.

This journey is a self-exploratory one. I don't know if we call it a memoir, or we call it some ideas and thoughts, but it is my own personal journey through my coaching, through the things that I had to go through, through me facing myself in the mirror and self-reflecting what my purpose was.

Whether I would be standing on a stage giving a speech, or in a leadership coaching session or with one person or with a group of people, or even if I were to be helping an entre-preneur develop a business, what I wanted to get out there is the message to help aspiring leaders and entrepreneurs going through a journey of self-awareness to embrace their authentic human leadership.

JOURNEYING TOWARDS AUTHENTIC HUMAN LEADERSHIP

This is how authentic human leadership emerges. The moment that we create more authentic human beings who are clear about their own values and willing to go through a journey of self-awareness to understand what has shaped them throughout the years, we are automatically making the world a better place. My personal purpose is to help in that. At the end of the book (do not jump into the last chapter) I genuinely share my own personal purpose, how it has come across and how I live it day by day.

Rest assured that your purpose will evolve throughout the years. It grows wings. However, as long as you feel that you're on this earth, trying to help others and making a difference in this world will create a ripple effect. This is how it all starts. We are human beings. We have the ability to support each other, help each other, embrace one another, create platforms for each other where we can support in the most authentic way.

My breakdown became my breakthrough.

My sleepless nights because of not being able to have clarity on the questions that were arising, or why I felt labelled by myself, were the exploration of the *real* me. I would like to take you on this journey with me, in my own way. I believe that we only heal by helping others. And in this book, *Without your job title, Who are you?*, I am putting myself out there to showcase vulnerability and present a personal journey, displaying the process that I had to go through. You may find you relate to the concept of my breakdown becoming my *breakthrough*.

In the next chapter, I will be talking about serendipity, which is one of my favourite words in English. We will explore the importance of self-reflection and our ability to transform our lives.

In Chapter 3, we will go deeper into the beliefs and their differences. Beliefs can either be limiting or empowering. Once we have clarity on them and how we can shift them, we become more empowered and understand why we do what we do.

In Chapter 4, we will be discussing strengths and weaknesses. We are born with natural talents and when we nurture them, we are able to perform a particular job with nearly flawless consistency over time.

After identifying our empowering beliefs and strengths development practice, we move, in Chapter 5, into the difference between Doing and Being. Moments of subconscious excellence can only occur during times of quiet, relaxation, or total inward concentration.

In Chapter 6, we explore how our actions are motivated by our values. Values serve as the foundation for all of the actions we take that are in line with them and help us develop and progress.

In Chapter 7, we consider the benefits of having a beginner's mindset and how exploring different options can help you feel more empowered. We explore deliberate practice benefits, when learning something new to us or when we want to improve on any skill.

This leads us to Chapter 8, where we explore how numerous aspects of our lives are affected by travel. Our current, enriching experiences have an effect on our creativity.

In Chapter 9, we navigate the connection between self-compassion and wellbeing, as well as its impact on our physical and emotional health.

In Chapter 10, we tap into the concept of leaning into our intuition as leaders, and how we can use this in our decision making. We explore some of the enemies of intuition and how not gathering the right proper perspective of any given situation can hinder us from taking the best decision.

In Chapter 11, we dive into why we are seeking a purpose in life and how studies have proven throughout the years that living a purposeful life has a great effect on us.

This leads us to the final Chapter which is empowerment of the self. The deepest core of true leadership is through empowerment, and empowerment starts with ourselves first.

The flow of the book enables you to read one chapter at a time, explore its actions, reflect on how it relates to you and practice some of the suggested calls to action that speak closely to you and your current stage of life.

CHAPTER 2

SERENDIPITY

FINDING SOMETHING GOOD WITHOUT LOOKING FOR IT

"It's no use going back to yesterday because I was a different person then." (Carroll, 2009) in Alice in Wonderland

What does this statement mean? Maybe we want to go back to a moment where things were completely different, or we were sometimes in a life-changing moment, or perhaps we want to return to something that was more enjoyable and fun, or we do not want to go back to something hurtful that has made us who we currently are. It could be that we have faced a big move or a big shift. We had a powerful breakdown. Whatever we have experienced, we change through the process.

Why? Because we become a different person. When we face anything that is super enjoyable and moments where things are fun, or when we face something that breaks us, we become someone different. Having to understand that I was a different person then meant I had gone through change and I had experienced growth, which is a natural part of our experience as human beings. We do not need to look at this as something that is negative in any form or stretch of the imagination, because change brings with it progress, resilience, memories, truth, and a lot of exploration. We might not be able to change the past absolutely, but life only happens for us when we are growing, and we are proactively trying to shift into better version of ourselves.

Why am I referring back to the idea of growth and development? It's because we learn a lot from yesterday and we learn a lot from things that we face. However, sometimes we don't have to wait until something good or bad happens in our lives in order for us to move into our aspired version of ourselves, we can already start to work on ourselves and equip ourselves with all the tools and the strengths that we currently have inside of us that can guide us into living a more content life, a life where we sense truthfulness, authenticity and fulfilment.

Move into the **ASPIRED** version of ourselves

Therefore, we can probably look at exploring the idea of the different forms of joy, and what joy means to us in our lives. When people look at the concept of joy, they are either looking at things that are outside of themselves in order for them to be able to feel that sense of joy or through someone or something else that gives them joy. However, even with joy being "a feeling of a great pleasure and happiness," it is limitless, and it is transformative input waiting to be tapped in each of us. We can always look into joy in ourselves and try to find it through lots of actions and self-exploration that can guide us into feeling joyful, into feeling grateful, into having fun, and into feeling contentment. This will automatically give us a sense of pride and helps us to foster a lot of relationships around us.

The different forms of joy are just there for us to tap into them, but we need to have a sense of exploration, authenticity, gratitude, love and respect. Joy is not only dependent on external factors. It's dependent on a mindset and a perspective shift and an emotional state that we need to practice and internally maintain. It is giving us this sense of freedom that when you feel that there is a young child inside you genuinely experiencing happiness, you know this is the type of joy that you are looking for and it's a journey that is worth exploring.

INNER DIMENSION

We all possess an inner dimension. This is where the magic happens and where we are genuinely vibrating at a level of happiness and contentment. We are able to discover peace and harmony in the inside work rather than focusing on the outer work. It is at this point that we essentially allow the extraordinary coincidence that occurs to us when we are open to possibilities, because we begin to perceive opportunities through a different set of eyes when we are viewing things from a perspective that is growth-oriented and that is promoting happiness.

When we look at things closely after getting new glasses, it's as though they are now cultivating. It's as if we just changed our glasses, and it is allowing us to inject more joy and happier moments into our lives. Things start to happen for us. For example, tap into these emotions that are not only based on negativity, but also about attracting and what we desire for the common good, and for the relationships that are around us. The first one is the relationship that we have with ourselves, and then the relationship that we have with other people around us, and how we can contribute more to our communities and to the world around us. It all has a ripple effect.

Science has proven that we are able to shift and change our mindset. There have been a lot of studies that have shown that through neuroplasticity and through changing our thoughts, there is a big possibility for us to change our lives. There have been a lot of books that have been written about how we can change the way that we think in order for us to be able to change the way that we live (Stanford University, 2021).

Wayne Dyer, the author of "Change your thoughts, Change your life" and "Your Erroneous Zones" has been one of the most inspirational authors and speakers in my life. Reading his wisdom and listening to his audios has forever changed my life. Dyer (2004) says: "Change the way you look at things and the things you look at change."

He also says that "Once you can change your thoughts, your new feelings will begin to emerge, and you will have taken the first step on the road to your personal freedom." (Dyer, 2007)

Dispenza (2013), has mentioned in his book, "Breaking the Habit of Being Yourself" that the knowledge that being oneself is all it takes to change one's thoughts, which leads to new experiences and new discoveries. He shares that, "What has profoundly and positively changed my life and the life of many others, is the understanding that changing one's mind – and thereby having new experiences and gaining new insights – is simply a matter of breaking the habit of oneself."

At this stage, it is important that we understand the two concepts of neuroplasticity and neurorigidity. In a neuroplasticity, this *plasticity* allows our actions to evolve and our behaviours to change, whereas neurorigidity is the inability to form new neural connections, living in the past without experiencing or learning new things. It is keeping the brain functioning in the same patterns while anticipating different outcomes.

Our brain cells can learn, and we are able to create and form new synaptic connections. Once these synaptic connections are made, we can shift our associations with everything in our mind to something entirely different. This is where we can grow and envision what our future may look like. How can we embrace the potential of our future in our lives?

Deepak Chopra™ (2022) founder of The Chopra Foundation named as the top 100 most influential people says: "Our minds influence the key activity of the brain, which in turn influences everything: perception, cognition, thoughts and feelings, personal relationships. They are all a projection of you."

Commitment and grit are also crucial factors in our willingness to pursue what we desire. I also relate commitment and grit to the types of goals we set for ourselves. Are we aiming for a specific outcome or focusing on the process? Most of the time, we fail to distinguish between these two objectives. Additionally, we often neglect to explain why we want to pursue something and whether it will bring internal or external benefits.

AUTHENTICITY CRISIS

This is, in a nutshell, a little reflection of us opening up to what the world is trying to shape us for. When I say the *world*, I mean our inner world. Do you sometimes not know who you are? When you lose the external thing that you've allowed to define you, like your job, a relationship, your finances, you can lose your sense of person and purpose. Trust me when I say that this is something that definitely can happen. It did happen to me, and it happened during the period of the pandemic when people were losing their jobs and were not able to clearly identify what should they do next, or what the new normal looked like. When people enter a period of crisis in their life, it creates uncertainty and confusion.

The problem was, for me, that my identity crisis was an *authenticity* crisis. I faced a personal conflict in understanding what I stood for, questioning my own purpose and passion in life, and what the traits were that influenced my own self-perception. Furthermore, how could I answer all these questions about myself, as well as work out what I wanted to stand for? This moment for me was an inner calling. I felt a huge void inside me. I felt I was feeling at odds with myself. I was feeling very anxious. I realised that I needed to find myself. I had lost myself somewhere. There were a lot of shifts in the way I looked at things. I changed my lifestyle from simply waking up and going to work to *owning* my morning. I tried to apply all the learning that I had gained throughout the years, from different speakers to different books. I was also supported by my coach.

Through self-reflection, meditation, sports and journaling, I began to integrate something new into my life. I also began learning new skills or methods of doing things. For example, I learned how to swim at the age of 39 and ultimately, I looked back on my story by writing this book and probably attempting to help myself by helping others. I discuss this in more detail in the following chapters. We heal by helping others. I always repeat this. Eventually, I hope that someone else will benefit from the shared knowledge I have in this work, as they travel their own path.

During the COVID-19 pandemic, many people faced numerous challenges, and it was a time filled with fear of the unknown. There were various signs of impact both during and after COVID-19. The pandemic had a significant effect on the workplace, and although there were some signs of recovery, the situation was even worse than in the first year of the pandemic. As a leader in my field, the primary factor that affected me was the workplace and the work environment. I witnessed significant changes in the industry, and it placed a heavy burden on me due to the actions taken by businesses worldwide, as well as the impact on everything I cherished, respected, and cared about.

EMOTIONAL WELLBEING

Employee wellbeing became the new work workplace initiative. Definitely, this has been looked into and employee engagement remains very low holding back enormous growth potential. Much of it is related to stress, to anger, and to the high levels of burnout at the workplace. Wellbeing influences their life at work.

This reflects on all the changes that have impacted us and the impact of work burnout on our lifestyle. Probably it was definitely the case before the pandemic; however, it has become apparent during the pandemic as this is the time when people needed to delve into their feelings about their work. They were no longer caught in the rat race of merely fulfilling their daily obligations without reflecting on their identity and values. Instead, they began aligning themselves to their company values and not their own values. The time during the pandemic allowed people to either thrive and understand, or go through an authenticity crisis like myself. It may have led them to embark on something entirely different, which, during this period, has made them battle or perhaps wonder, "Okay, what's next for me?"

An authenticity crisis is a crisis. It is a crisis of understanding.

Why do you feel what you're feeling? Why are you not comfortable? Why are you feeling there is something more to be explored? Why do you want to stand up for what is going on around you? You start to question so many things.

One important question, a highlight for me, is, *"Why am I doing what I'm doing? What is my unique value or contribution to my own personal brand as a human being?"*

An authenticity crisis
is a crisis of
UNDERSTANDING.

This journey entails emotional restraints. It has its own path toward growth, but it also has pain points along the way that force us to stop and think about how we may occasionally be experiencing feelings of burnout.

Wellbeing is currently something many companies are currently looking at, but doing meaningful work is an important part of living a fulfilling life.

Let us reflect back on wellbeing in careers, because during the pandemic, people's careers were impacted. They didn't have a strong system outside of their wellbeing since so many people were working a lot and their work was just a reflection of who they were, and hence it had an impact on everything else in their lives. When it comes to our social interaction, we lost our way. There was also a financial impact on many.

Because the pillars of my life have always been around my work and who I am, when one of those pillars were shaking, everything else did as well. This has made me want to speak about the impact of self-leadership and the impact of poor self-leadership, because it all started with me not having an understanding of my own self.

R.E.A.D.

In the upcoming chapters, I will be speaking about different subjects, and I encourage you to go through them in the form called R.E.A.D.

- R stands for Reflect.
- E stands for Explore.
- A stands for Advance.
- D stands for Develop.

Although during the pandemic, we were all under the impression, or at least myself, that the problem was COVID, the problem was deeper than COVID. Problems sometimes disguise themselves in different forms. For me, and now that I had enough time to think about what was happening around me, I have a full understanding of those emotions at that time.

Although my job wasn't impacted during that period, I continued asking myself: Who am I and what do I stand for? And if I don't have this job, WHO AM I?

REFLECT

I had to do a lot of self-reflection. I needed to move past my fear of the known into the unknown ask questions like: What is next for me? What do I represent as a human being? What do I stand for? This was the time to Reflect. Not everyone needs to go through a crisis or something similar in order for them to be able to go through a reflection process. They could just be living a content life and wanting to reflect on what is going on, because they have a growth mindset and they want develop and equip themselves with the right tools that could help them fulfill their dreams, live a meaningful life, improve their wellbeing, or probably foster some of the relationships that they have with others.

EXPLORE

Let us go through what I mean by explore. It is about identifying the story that we've been telling ourselves and looking at what is limiting us from moving into the next stages. Thus, we need to explore the concept of limiting beliefs. We also explore getting clarity on our talents, strengths, and how to cultivate them, going through a journey towards our values and juggling between the to-do list and the to-be list. This is a kind of exploration into different areas of ourselves that can help us get an insight on what we represent.

ADVANCE

Now let's dive into advance, which is the A of R.E.A.D. This is where we unlearn and re-learn. We speak about the importance of learning new things in our lives and the beginner's mindset that we can apply. We speak to a dear topic of mine, which is travelling and its connection to us, living in a world where everything is open to us and how this can cultivate a feeling of wellbeing to us. Practicing self-compassion, which is a subject that we do not always speak about because we tend to focus more on resilience. Further, we are probably compassionate with people around us, but not with ourselves and raising our level of intuition.

DEVELOP

Now we are ready to Develop. We will be talking about purpose and possibility, and self-leadership. Once we have clarity on our purposeful possibility guided by a high level of self-leadership, we move through our lives with more impact and alignment.

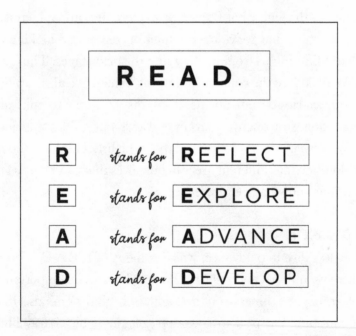

I repeat, most of the parts of this book are probably a short memoir, because I write from the experience of what I have faced and what I have done in order for me to be able to identify more of who am I as a person and what I stand for, without me being impacted by a title. This has shaped me into a change-maker, the person that I aspire to be, which is a human being that creates impact and who gives back to the community, trying to live a fulfilling life.

This is where the word Serendipity comes through, because "finding something good without looking for it" was my authenticity crisis. My breakdown during the pandemic was my blessing. It was my serendipity. Serendipity is now not only my favourite word in the English language but my blessing in disguise.

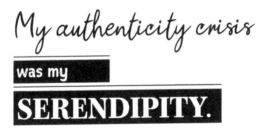

The key takeaways from this is to be open minded to all the ideas that will come across. You might have a great connection with some of the thoughts that are there, or some "Aha!" moments for others, and you might say it does not make sense. Having an open mind in understanding the opportunity that you're ready for, is key. You will only notice your opportunities once you have peeled back the layers that stop you from being ready for your next authentic self, because there is inside you a person who is very strong, a person wanting to grow and develop. There is a person inside you that is wanting to become the change-maker they aspire to be.

I am only sharing my journey here, which is a reflection of my own ideas, experiences, actions, and behavioural changes. I am no guru. I am no person who says, "Yes, I got it, and that is all." I am still work in progress. I still struggle to apply a few things when life gets busy, but I realign myself, and at the end of the day, I am a human being having a growth mindset towards a purposeful life. It only takes one person to change your life, and that person is you. In most of the chapters, you will see a lot of practical tools to implement the topics that I am talking about.

I look forward to sharing my insights with you in the upcoming chapters. I hope my story will guide you on your own personal journey to unfold your true potential and to live a purposeful life. All your dreams are a purposeful possibility waiting to be lived.

ALL YOUR DREAMS

ARE A PURPOSEFUL
POSSIBILITY
waiting to be lived.

CHAPTER 3

SCOLIOSIS

WE ARE NOT BROKEN, JUST BENT

Have you ever thought of words that start with your own initials? For me, I choose the following. Of course, I choose serendipity as now you know that it is one of my favourite words and S is for scoliosis. I have known that I have Scoliosis since I was young.

For those who do not know what scoliosis means, it is where the spine twists and curves to the side. It can affect people of any age, from babies to adults, but most often starts in children aged 10 to 15. Sometimes you need to go through a certain medical treatment. It doesn't have to mean that it's very serious. There are different types. It could be mild and sometimes it could lead to a surgery that could affect the body. We're not going to have a scientific study here about scoliosis. However, I want you to know that you should never be ashamed of your own story, because you never know how it could help others.

By the end of this chapter, you will learn about something that is called limiting beliefs. They could be called disempowering beliefs or limiting thoughts about the self. Some people call them restrictive beliefs. You can call it whatever you want. I call them limiting belief because I personally believe that some of these beliefs are what shape us. They are impacting us through past experiences, environments, events that happen, and the limiting beliefs are the story we tell ourselves or we *choose* to tell ourselves when we are doing anything or when we want to come up with a decision.

It is time for you to reframe your story and then rethink what have you been telling yourself throughout these years. Because what you have been telling yourself throughout these years is something that has brought you to where you are currently today. You might be wondering what scoliosis has to do with it. Let me tell you a story about something that happened in my childhood. I was a child who had been diagnosed with scoliosis at a very young age. I don't remember whether I was eight or nine or ten, but I remember that I was a child. My grandma from my mother's side who was quite loving and not in any way trying to embed consciously any limiting beliefs or any limiting thoughts into my head, was talking to another lady. They were both in the hospital because they were doing kidney distillation, and I used to go with my grandma and my mum because we wanted to take her back to the house afterwards. They sat there for a couple of hours.

They started a conversation about me and my new diagnosis of scoliosis.

Grandma: "Her spinal cord is not straight. She has scoliosis. The doctor said they need to do some exercises, so it doesn't get worse."

Lady: "Does this mean she is abnormal? Do not tell anybody that she has this in her spinal cord. Men might not even want to marry her."

Whilst the conversation was just a casual chat between two ladies (bless their souls!), it is clear what impact it might have had on a child like myself. Thank God that I had a strong will and this didn't impact me personally throughout the years. I grew adapting to my scoliosis. Now my yoga teacher keeps on telling me, "Your scoliosis is a gift because you can bend" and my fitness coach tells me, "You just have to realign." It made me feel very special because in any activity I had to do, they would always suggest some inversions, and this also led me to learn swimming, which we are going to be talking about it in the next chapters. It hasn't stopped me from doing many things that I wanted to do as I was growing up.

THE STORIES WE TELL OURSELVES

What we listen to as children and as adults can be shaped into the stories that can become the reasons of our limiting beliefs. My level of understanding about the subject was very easy. Throughout the years, I have had different opinions about myself where I would be hearing something or somebody at work that might have made a comment which got stuck in my head. However, our limiting beliefs come up from interactions like the ones that my grandma had in this discussion or maybe your teacher, your friend, anyone, when you hear somebody saying like, *"They're not smart,"* or *"You are not good,"* or *"You are not able to do this thing,"* or *"Science is not for you,"* etc.

We are shaped through growing up with these types of beliefs. They are what make us. If I had listened to the story that this lady said, I might have thought that I am not normal. I would not have had any confidence and throughout the years I've had my journey of facing some of the beliefs that shaped me. People speak to their mindset or level of understanding about the topic, not necessarily to the truth. You have to always remember that.

THE STORIES we tell ourselves

We're going to be talking about how we deal with this mindset, and how we are able to reframe our limiting beliefs and turn them into empowering beliefs.

We think that these types of beliefs are real. These thoughts and the beliefs that we have are deep-seated beliefs that affect our lives, but they often go unrecognised because we are programmed throughout the years. Our limiting beliefs act as unconscious thoughts that become a defence mechanism, and we might be angry or sad or anxious or frustrated, or go into something that I call low vibrating emotions. When we go into low vibrating emotions, it is because there has been a belief that has triggered something that has made us suffer in the past. We use these limiting beliefs as a defence mechanism because they're unconscious.

But is it real? And if it is real or it is proven to be real, what are you going to do about it? Whether you think that having a limiting belief is a good thing or not, how can you change it to an empowering belief? These limiting beliefs are underlying. I call them "underlying" because they are under the surface of *our behaviours and our emotions. Limiting beliefs are when you say to yourself*:

"I don't know how to do this."

"I don't have time."

"I am not attractive."

"Everyone else is better at their job than I am."

"I am too young to be a manager."

"I don't have enough experience."

"I am unable to lead this meeting."

"Everyone just wants to take and never give."

"The world is full of selfish people."

These are beliefs that have stemmed from times in life when you have been faced with consecutive actions that have led you to believe that there are people who are always selfish, or someone told you that you are not good enough.

This doesn't mean that everybody is selfish. It is what you choose to tell yourself and you've believed it throughout the years. It is as simple as that. If I choose to tell myself, "I am unattractive" because somebody, maybe in a relationship, has once told me "you are unattractive" and at that moment I had a feeling of frustration or a very sad emotion or low self-worth, that incident sometimes shapes itself into a limiting belief.

When you say, "I am always busy, I don't have time," to a passion or hobby of yours that you want to practice because you have believed that you are probably not good enough, there is always a subconscious, underlying reason that has caused you this belief.

Many people have spoken about this limiting, underlying belief, but what I want to refer to is that we generally choose to ignore these limiting beliefs.

Take a moment to look into yourself now and just think of one idea that you have believed throughout your life because of something that has happened in the past. I guarantee you; you will have two or three that will pop up directly into your mind. It is there. It is in your subconscious and being used as a defence mechanism. It has affected your life. But what are you going to do about it? Are you going to just sit there and say, "I don't know how to do this and because I don't know how to do this, I'm not going to take the time to learn it?"

Dweck (2007) in her book *Mindset: The New Psychology of Success* show us that the way we think, both consciously and unconsciously, influences us and even simple things like how we express ourselves can greatly impact our personal growth. Dweck's research demonstrates the influence of our fundamental beliefs, revealing the substantial impact they have on our mindset. Our perception of our own personalities plays a significant role in determining our potential, both motivating and limiting us in our pursuit of success.

She writes *"Sure, people with the fixed mindset have read the books that say: Success is about being your best self, not about being better than others; failure is an opportunity, not a condemnation; effort is the key to success. But they can't put this into practice because their basic mindset–their belief in fixed traits–is telling them something entirely different: that success is about being more gifted than others, that failure does measure you, and that effort is for those who can't make it on talent."* (Dweck, 2007)

Here are some questions that will help you look at the beliefs you hold about yourself, about other people, and the whole world around you.

- *What am I holding?*
- *In what areas am I waiting for someone else to take the responsibility for me?*
- *In what ways am I allowing the fear of change to hold me back from moving forward into my life?*
- *In what ways do I consider I am not deserving or self-worthy?*
- *In what areas am I spending too much time on things that are not my own priorities?*
- *In what areas do I need to learn or further develop my skills in order to get ahead in life?*
- *What consistent negative patterns do I have about myself?*

Take a pause, reflect on this. Knowing that you may change over time makes you more willing to examine, learn from, and develop from difficulties. These beliefs have been sabotaging your self-development.

THE EMPOWERING BELIEFS

In the TED talk "The Power of Believing You Can Improve" Dweck explains what they did with students by saying: *"In one study, we taught them that every time they push out of their comfort zone to learn something new and difficult, the neurons in their brain can form new, stronger connections, and over time they can get smarter. ... students who were not taught this growth mindset continued to show declining grades over this difficult school transition, but those who were taught this lesson showed a sharp rebound in their grades. We have shown this now, this kind of improvement, with thousands and thousands of kids, especially struggling students."* (Street, 2021)

This can be done through deliberate practice, which is a universal approach. Ericsson and Pool (2017) mention in the book *Peak: Secrets from the New Science of Expertise*, the following: *"With deliberate practice, however, the goal is not just to reach your potential but to build it, to make things possible that were not possible before. This requires challenging homeostasis–getting out of your comfort zone–and forcing your brain or your body to adapt."*

There are plenty of these limiting beliefs in your head, but these limiting beliefs can definitely become more empowering. You can use them as self-reflection tools to empower yourself. Take time to answer the above questions I have asked and reflect back on what you have been telling yourself throughout these years.

My story throughout the coaching journey has been, "What would people think if I failed as a coach?" Another aspect is reflecting on why this important to me, because there have been some limiting beliefs that have been embedded in my head throughout my life. These have to do with the fact that I believed people's opinion of me mattered. I have worked hard to achieve the position that I am currently in, and I am considered as somebody who is reputable and who has authority in the industry. If I explore a skillset in a different industry, what would people think? Digging deep inside, this really didn't matter to me, but I have unconsciously been unaware of it.

Those who know me well know that I have a passionate love for photography and we're going to talk about that a little bit later, but I've never tried painting. The first time I went to a painting class, it was a birthday gift from my friend. I thought to myself, "I do not know how to paint." I have been told that if you are somebody who is so much into business and numbers, your creative part is not there. However, I've been practicing photography for many years, and it helps me when I need to unwind. It was something that I enjoyed. My relationship with my camera was very good. Previously, I believed that I could not go into anything creative, but I did it with photography.

Again, the thoughts popped in my head: "You cannot be creative if you are in business or if you are somebody who has not done something in the past. Photography is different as it is technical also." I didn't allow it to stop me. I enjoyed painting and it became a hobby. Every time I went to a session, I felt I was getting better and better at it. It was helping me to find my deeper creative side. I am glad I pushed through this belief to find something that I love.

Let us explore another belief: "Everybody wants to take and never give." This is a very harsh, strong belief shaped by interactions with people who have not been the most generous with us, or perhaps we have given more to them that they have given back. However, how is this belief serving us? If we start our relationship with anyone, whether a romantic connection, a friend or a colleague, and we put a label of the sort, we are going to go into the relationship with doubt. We're not going to have trust and not having trust does not serve us. We are not tuning into humanity because these limiting beliefs are stopping us from knowing the truth about the people who are around us.

How many times have you told yourself: "I am not good at this?" What would the worst-case scenario be? If you failed at it, what would happen? Nothing. What we care about sometimes is nothing more than us trying to judge ourselves. Go into what is the truth. Go into the story of your limitless beauty and you unable to dig into this human-empowered belief that you have inside you. Change your fixed mindset to growth mindset.

I had a client who had an understanding throughout the years that in order for you to be successful in the entertainment business, you need to remain young. It is the story that they have been told, because somebody at some point has implied that growing older in the entertainment business means no one will choose to hire you.

My answer was: "Have you seen J. Lo at some point recently? She looks younger than me. She has limitless beauty. She's been working on herself throughout the years and she's shining as she grows older." Of course, we had to dig into the reasons why we have been saying this to ourselves and how this can be reframed, and how can we embrace gracefulness as we grow older. The thought of "Getting older" was shifted into

"Limitless beauty." The story has completely changed. The client was able to be in touch with her own truth.

When a friend of mine was having a discussion with me about a project that she wanted to put out but was worried about what people would think, we dipped into this limiting belief together. We identified that, at some point in her career in the past, she put together a project and it didn't work out. At that time, she was convinced that everybody who was watching her has seen her fail. The emotions of failure resurfaced because she was worried about what people would think.

We dug into the worst-case scenario. We looked into the belief she held, which was just hers and no one else's. We explored the emotion and the level of mindset about projects. We wrote down this limiting belief and we reframed it. We reframed it into an empowering belief. We noticed that she was putting all her energy into thoughts around what might happen if she would fail, instead of focusing on all the creativity and the action to launch the project. She moved her energy and pivoted into something that was more along the lines of: What if I did not fail? If failure was not an option, her creativity developed. She's one of the most successful people I currently know. She made peace with a failure that was only in her head.

For this to work for you, you need to be willing to put energy into it. You need to invest your energy into taking action when you believe that it'll produce results. You need to be willing to take a different approach instead of the current limiting belief. Go back to the questions and spend time on them. Ask yourself: "What is my new empowering story? If I didn't have this belief, what would be different? If this didn't exist, how would I shine? How would I step into my empowerment?"

I encourage you to look into empowering affirmations. Affirmations frame what I want to tell myself every single day. This is not just positive talk. Affirmations are an assertion that something exists, or something is true. Replace your limiting disempowering beliefs with empowering affirmations as a first step. If you've been telling yourself, "I am bad at this," then tell yourself, "I am successful. I am confident. I am powerful. I am strong. I am getting better and better every day. I am filled with focus. I can do whatever I want to do, or I can be whatever I want to be. I am constantly growing and evolving into a better person. I am healing and strengthening every single day."

Tell that to yourself when these limiting beliefs come creeping in your head. My coach calls them saboteurs. They come up just to talk and talk and talk and talk in our head and say, "I am not good."

You can disempower those limiting beliefs through empowering affirmations, through going into your self and identifying them. Empowering affirmations eat away the saboteurs.

DISEMPOWER those limiting beliefs *through* **EMPOWERING AFFIRMATIONS.**

Gratitude gets rid of these limiting beliefs. If you embrace gratitude and you are grateful of your current situation, your whole energy will change.

Can you imagine the level of energy that is going through you when you are changing your limiting beliefs, digging into yourself and identifying them? When excuses come, ask yourself, "Is it true or is it a limiting belief?" Putting it into perspective is a great way of doing that. When this idea surfaces, ask yourself, "Why am I feeling what I'm feeling and what action I should take to go into a goal-directed thinking?" As Tony Robbins says, "If people maintain the belief systems that empower them, they'll keep coming back with enough action and enough resourcefulness to succeed eventually."

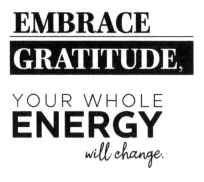

CALL to CHANGE

Let's take a moment to look at this self-reflection exercise. It is crucial that we understand how our set of mistaken limiting beliefs came about before we can go into reprogramming ourselves with more supportive beliefs and more functional ones.

1. Take time to reflect and consider any limiting beliefs that you may be holding inside you.
2. Write them down.
3. Answer the below set of questions about each belief you have written down.

   a. *Is this belief always true about me or occasionally?*
   b. *What is the evidence that this belief is always true or not?*
   c. *Does this belief serve me and encourage my own wellbeing?*
   d. *Does this limiting belief consider the big picture or not?*
   e. *Is this limiting belief a choice of mine?*
   f. *Is this limiting belief something that has been influenced by my family or friends or co-workers?*
   g. *Has this limiting belief come up in my life as I was growing up?*
   h. *What are the consequences of this belief?*
   i. *What is holding on this belief costing me?*
   j. *What is the evidence I have against this belief?*

4. How can I rewrite my limiting belief into an empowering and serving one? What is the alternative statement,
   counterstatement, empowering statement, or self-changing
   statement I can start using today to start changing this limiting belief?

This is an exercise that you can do for one belief, or many.
You can always go back to it when you feel that you are having
some beliefs that are hindering you or your progress.

This leads me to talk about individuality of each and every one
of us and how we are all unique in our own ways.

CHAPTER 4

RUBIK'S CUBE

YOU ARE LIKE A RUBIK'S CUBE, SIMPLE YET COMPLEX, A POTENTIAL THAT CONTINUES TO UNLOCK

Being a huge fan of Will Smith, and I don't know if you remember the scene from the movie, *The Pursuit of Happyness*, 2006. (Gardner & Muccino, 2006)

In short, the movie was starring Will Smith as Chris Gardner, a homeless salesman, who was hustling to pay his rent and has been struggling to perform his sales job selling a bone density scanner. He had his wife and a son to take care of.

One day, he has a conversation with a man on the street, who happens to be a stockbroker, and in the conversation, Chris asks him two questions, "What do you do and how do you do it?" The man responds to Chris that he's a stockbroker, and then Chris asks him, "You have to go to college to be a stockbroker, right?" The man says, "No, not necessarily. You just have to be good with numbers and good with people."

The focus now for Chris was to be able to apply for an internship at the stockbroker firm, even if he had not the experience for a college degree and he knew that his application would not be considered. But he wanted a way to showcase to Jay his potential. He goes in a cab with Jay trying to convince him that he is good at handling tough situations, but Jay is hardly listening to Chris and busy solving a Rubik's cube. At that time, a Rubik's cube was a common sight on TV and people were trying to solve it.

Chris proclaims to Jay that he can solve it, and he hands over the Rubik's cube to him. The cab driver even looks at Chris sarcastically, and Jay is not even convinced that he could do it, but still hands it over. By the time they reached to the destination, Chris had already solved the Rubik's cube. Surprised and impressed by Chris's ability to solve it, Chris lands an interview at the firm and the story continues from there.

What does the Rubik's Cube represent? Why am I talking about it? Is it us with all our different sides? Is it the obstacles that you put yourself into? Is it the possibilities?

We can relate to a Rubik's cube in many different ways. The Rubik's cube can represent obstacles, but it can also represent talent. It can represent your uniqueness. We have the power to refuse to be labelled as one colour or one side. Like a Rubik's cube we can be a combination of colours and sides. We are a mix of strengths. We are unique.

However, the complex situation is that there will always be a simplification to it. Keep calm and play it well. Play it like a Rubik's cube.

Think about a time where perseverance was the only way for you to continue and be driven. How did you feel back then? What was the energy that you experienced? What were the thoughts that you had? What did you lean onto?

Do you know that you have a set of talents, capabilities and strengths that have helped you at a specific situation? Have you ever reflected on that?

We are all like a Rubik's cube. We are probably trying to label ourselves as one probably side or colour of the Rubik's cube, but we are more talented than that. We are more driven by a certain set of skills that has brought us to where we are today. Do you know that? You have definitely leaned on your own capabilities throughout the years.

We have covered in the previous chapter the limiting beliefs. It is our nature to critique ourselves, a nature we develop throughout years of self-judgment or of growing and being programmed by certain comments and certain words that we have been told. Imagine the power of these words. Imagine the power of the words that have been told to you, that have developed into limiting beliefs, that have shaped you into who you are today.

What we are trained to do is to follow the conventional way of development whenever we want to focus on something. Remember the last time that you were in school, when you were not good at a language or any subject, and they would always give you a teacher to get better at it.

But how might this benefit you if they gave you a teacher for a subject you were best at? Imagine you were excelling in math, but probably not very good in English literature. The very natural thing that the parents usually do is that they bring you a teacher or tutor for English. I mean, you definitely need to know English. It's the most well-known language in the world, but at the same time, what if they had also supported you with a math teacher? You may have excelled at that. What we tend to do is always focus on something that we are not good at. You can still have both teachers. Why not? You can excel and get better at something else. We have just mentioned earlier that through deliberate practice, you can improve from point A to point B, but instead we focus our efforts on trying to fix our weaknesses.

If we continue putting effort and spending our lives trying to fix our weaknesses, we will not get too far. We will probably prevent failure, but we will not get too far. We will not achieve our highest potential. We will only see mediocre progress.

INNATE ABILITY

Talent is the innate ability and inner trait that naturally manifests. It is what comes easily to you and what you are most likely to do. You are a born leader. When you do anything, it affects the way you feel, how you think, and how you act.

A skill is a learned talent that is developed by practice, official and informal training, or both.

Knowledge is what you know. It is acquired through formal or informal learning.

Your strengths should typically be abilities that are reinforced by experience. If communication is one of your strengths, for instance, think back to a time when you utilised it to accomplish a task or solve an issue.

Strengths and skills may be distinguished clearly. People learn, develop, and grow better at skills through time and with practice. Strengths, on the other hand, are capabilities that a person has naturally.

People who are aware of their talents are better able to appreciate what makes them special and how their personalities affect their team. Knowing your talents contributes to developing self-awareness. It might help you rediscover qualities about yourself that you have previously disregarded.

Knowing your natural abilities better will enable you to find and seize opportunities that will enable you to consistently perform at your best, allowing you to develop your undeveloped gifts into strengths and reach your full potential.

MY DREAM TALENT

The first step is that you have to learn what your natural talents are so you can start developing them. This comes through awareness about these talents, the skills, the blind spots and how you can apply them to your daily life.

Was there some hobby that you always wanted to practice but you didn't because you had no time or you thought you cannot do it? What are some things that you always notice that you do naturally?

When you are receiving feedback from your seniors, most of the time it focuses on areas of development, but what happens to the areas of strengths, what you do well? It gets taken for granted.

I am not saying we don't have to work on the areas of opportunity for us but what if we leverage on what we do best?

When I was a young girl, I always wanted to play the guitar. My parents wanted me to play the piano. I loved the piano. It was dreamy and now I enjoy listening to it. They even bought me a keyboard. I was practicing with my teacher, but the teacher was a bit harsh, and the keys of the keyboard versus the piano are different as the piano is stronger so even my home practice wasn't serving me much. I used to dislike my teacher's comments and I ended up quitting because the feedback was only focusing on what I was not doing right. I ended up not playing the guitar or the piano. If my parents had had the awareness of talent I am talking about here, I could now be playing the guitar or even both. It is important to listen to what we feel naturally drawn towards.

CLARITY

Clarity on my own abilities and skills has helped me throughout the years because whenever I have opened hotels or when I have been in charge of certain projects, it was very easy for me to identify the different individual talents and what makes people tick. I've worked very hard on ensuring that I always developed winning teams, and having winning teams means having individuals who are unique and different and can blend together for the greater good.

CLARITY *on my own*
ABILITIES & SKILLS
has helped me throughout the years.

Never undervalue who you are. It involves making a realistic assessment of your talent, abilities, and skills. That doesn't call for arrogant behaviour. While some people undoubtedly exaggerate or overestimate their abilities, the majority err on the side of discarding them too quickly. We might have been pushed away from them in the past. Is your natural talent in arts or sports but you never practiced it?

Therefore, ask yourself:

What are you excellent at that people keep pointing out to you?

What are skills that people keep asking for your help with?

Where do people compliment you the most?

Even if it may not be what you want to be remembered for, you can use any ability or strength to help you achieve your goals. Utilizing them helps you better understand who you are as a leader and your own brand.

Go back to the activities you enjoyed doing as a child. You will find so many answers there.

For this to work, you have to believe that our talent doesn't label us. We are the sum of combined unique gifts, our differences as humans are our resources. There is no bad or good talent. You know what you are good at, but if you wanted to find the best way for you to lead a purposeful life is to have an opportunity to work with others by connecting with them and appreciate the differences and gaining greater self-awareness.

Let's go back to Chris Gardner who said, "Remember that you got to dream, you got to protect it. People can do something themselves. They want to tell you what you cannot do. If you want something, go get it, period." (Gardner & Muccino, 2006)

You have the tools inside you to achieve your dreams. All you need is to have clarity on them and investment in applying them. When we potentially apply our talents, they can become a greater source of fulfillment. We become more confident, happy, energetic, and likely to achieve our goals.

Solve your own Rubik's cube, transform your great potential into great performance. Ask yourself, how do I identify what do I do best? How can I use my talents to accomplish what is most important for me? What are my unique contributions?

This serves as a starting point to your self-discovery. This serves into your self-discovery, absolutely. It also will be a step for you to look at what have you been doing so far in your life. In the next chapter, we are going to be talking more about doing versus being.

CALL *to* DISCOVER

- Look for a few instances in your life where you have been your most natural self in working or in personal life, going full-flow with your natural abilities and feeling good in your flow.
- What were the superpowers you used in these situations? List them.
- Are your able to identify some patterns? You might notice that the overlapping skills are your talents.
- Answer the below questions:
  - What comes naturally to you or looks easy to you?
  - When do you feel like you're "in the flow"?
  - What kinds of issues do you like to solve?
  - What do individuals want you to assist them with?
  - What extra responsibilities have you accepted at work only because you like them?
  - What expertise and abilities have you acquired throughout the course of your career?
  - What expertise and abilities have you acquired in your personal life?
  - What activities did you engage in as a child?
  - What aspects of yourself do you love?
  - When do you feel your best, whether it's at work or in your personal life?

I also encourage you to look for online assessment talents or strengths tests that can identify your personal qualities and guide you in the right direction.

This leads us to doing and being.

CHAPTER 5

DOING OR BEING?

"DOING IS NEVER ENOUGH IF YOU NEGLECT BEING." (TOLLE, 2008)

Have you ever felt that you are in a rat race? You are trying to improve the quality of your life by doing more, by accumulating more, by demonstrating a high level of success, but you still feel that you have a very high level of burnout which keeps you at the same pace? However, you don't understand that this rat race does not have any finish line. It will keep on spinning and spinning and spinning and you forget to stand, evaluate, or realise what are the real stressors that are instilling in you this to-do attitude the whole time. Being in the rat race has probably given you some level of satisfaction but we have to remember that we are not a *human doing*, we are *human being*.

Dyer (2009) said, "I am a human being, not a human doing. Don't equate yourself worth with how well you do things in life. You aren't what you do. If you are what you do, then when you don't, you are not." We are associating ourselves with a job, a title, a list of to-do things that sometimes if we're not doing this it may mean we are probably not being, and this is kind of a dangerous zone for us to be in. In simple words, doing, being, which is also wellbeing, is simple in terms. Wellbeing means being well, which can be written this way: BE-ing well. Most of the time we forget the word BE. What does it mean to just be?

Too many of us in this planet exist in a waking sleep. We are mindful. We are not feeding from an empty cup. We take good care of themselves. We are being. Doing is our default mode. It is linked to action, whereas being is linked to our awareness mode. It is linked to our connection with our present moment and the present moment is the only moment that exists. Your past has already gone, your future is yet to be, but your present moment is only now, and your future was once your present moment. From the moment you started to read this chapter until now, it was passed. It's a very powerful way to look at being.

Let me share with you my own story. It was in December 2019 when my friend introduced me to an online meditation group. The meditation was a 21 days meditation challenge for abundance. We were receiving the abundance meditation and exercises every single day.

I loved the reflection exercises, and it was one of my first experiences with this type of meditation and combined with some inner reflection. One day we had to do an exercise where we needed to write the below statement: "I, Soumana Ammar, completely forgive myself for not seeing my own (vulnerability)." Vulnerability, oh my God, this word hit me. It was so deep. It hit me deep. I needed to know more about myself. Why I am always resilient and feel there was a deeper sense to what I want to do. I realised I needed to BE more.

I COMPLETELY
FORGIVE
M Y S E L F
for not seeing my own
VULNERABILITY

We navigate through life with an autopilot operating system that impacts our feelings, stressors like doubt, anger, resentment, and suffering. Then we become tuned in to emotional cravings, and our past experiences reaffirm these emotions. As you might have heard, we are constantly busy being busy.

Can you imagine that? It's like we crave emotional stimulation because we keep ourselves occupied. It's an emotional craving for busyness.

However, being busy doesn't always mean being productive or purposeful. Sometimes we are simply busy because we don't want to take the time to sit with ourselves and reflect. Many people are afraid of spending time alone because they are worried about what might come up. In reality, everyone is constantly working through a to-do list. They chase after this list because they are chasing something else. Refusing to escape from the cycle of to-do lists is a phenomenon that has persisted for many years. This is why when the pandemic hit, it caused high levels of stress for everyone. People were deeply entrenched in their busyness and couldn't comprehend what was happening when they were forced to stop.

BEING
BUSY
doesn't always mean

BEING
PRODUCTIVE *or*
PURPOSEFUL

The sudden change in direction disrupted their programmed routines and had a profound impact on them. For some people, the pandemic was an opportunity to finally pause. When we are caught up in a busy, stressful life filled with commitments and packed schedules, we tend to neglect introspection. We only focus on the external aspects of our lives. This is how we become stuck in repetitive patterns and hinder our personal growth.

When we are fixated on doing, we become consumed by career goals, life goals, and demanding projects. We are tempted to prioritise action and lose sight of everything else, including our health and well-being. We neglect our hobbies and disregard our passions. As a result, our inner resources become depleted, leaving us feeling drained and exhausted. In my opinion, when it comes to change, the statement "Nothing changes if nothing changes" holds true. If you continue doing the same things, you should expect the same results.

During a training session at the hotel, where I often teach colleagues about consistency, I use a metaphor involving two cups of water. I explain that if you add one spoonful of sugar to each glass of water, which are both at the same level and contain the same amount of millilitres, the sweetness of the water will be the same. However, if you decide to add half a glass of sugar to one cup and perhaps two glasses of sugar to the other, the sweetness will differ. This is where inconsistencies arise. When we adhere to standards, we strive for consistency. However, when you want to bring about change in your life, you must decide what you want to pour into your cup.

WELLBEING DIMENSIONS

Wellbeing has many dimensions. Some of them are physical, emotional, spiritual, financial, social, environmental, and intellectual. They vary in the terms of their level of contentment from one person to the other. You could be content in your emotional wellbeing but not content in your physical wellbeing. You could be content in your financial wellbeing but very tired in terms of your physical wellbeing. You could be very content with your social wellbeing, but you are unable to make any progress in your intellectual wellbeing because you're busy socialising. The list goes on and on and on.

Mindfulness plays an impactful role in all of these dimensions. To be able to assess how well you are in any of these dimensions, you need to be mindful of them in the first place and have your own definition of what they mean to you and, secondly, you also need to evaluate where do you stand in each of them. Wellbeing refers to the person's ability to live a life that they value.

Once you know how you are in these dimensions and you know at what level or value these dimensions are in your life, you can evaluate your level of contentment in them. How content am I in my physical dimension, emotional dimension, etc. With the clarity on the levels of the dimensions, this is where we need to take mindful decisions and actions of doing to shift towards a better wellbeing. Take time to ask yourself and assess your level of satisfaction in all the above dimensions. In every moment you have an opportunity to ask yourself whether your way of being is empowering you or not.

You have heard me speak about empowering beliefs in the previous chapters and now we are talking about the empowering level of dimensions and empowering actions that are associated with it. Empowering, because you have the power in you. You just have to be mindful about it. A powerful step that could take you to shift into being mode is to stop and ask yourselves the below questions: Who am I being right now? Does that serve me? If not, then who and how do I want to be?

EMPOWERING,

because you have

THE POWER IN YOU.

You just have to be

MINDFUL ABOUT IT.

As easy as it sounds, some people can take time to answer these questions because we do not know what we want to be in order for us to be at our potential wellbeing. As I mentioned, the importance placed on the above dimensions will vary from one person to another. However, if we can maintain an element of focus in all areas and dimensions of our lives, we will be more likely to achieve a healthier life balance. The idea is not to stop fully doing. It is to achieve a balance between doing and being so you're able to understand your actions, the decisions that you are taking, and also to allow new ideas to come and guide you towards your purpose.

Don't postpone it to next year. Don't postpone it to next month. Don't postpone it to tomorrow. Don't postpone it to this afternoon. Give yourself the time for you to spend on being, on reflecting, on understanding where you stand in this compass of your inner guidance. Where do you stand with these dimensions? How satisfied are you with the current dimensions that you have in your life? Spend some time.

SUBCONSCIOUS EXCELLENCE

Moments of subconscious excellence, they only come from moments of silence, or relaxation, or a complete inner focus. This is how I was inspired to write this book.

When I wrote the article on LinkedIn, *Who are you without your job title?* (This was the actual title), it became such a successful post that it exceeded more than 180,000 views, and that was only because I had clarity. I was not sure on why it came out of me, but it was after a meditation that morning where I felt I needed to write that. I thought to myself: I refuse the labels we put on people. I've been thinking about the subject for almost a week. We put labels on ourselves, and we perform actions thinking that they align with how we are supposed to live our lives. Inside each of us there is a compass, there is an inner guidance. It was the reason why I'm currently writing this book. If I hadn't taken the time to sit in silence and go within during my meditation, I wouldn't have understood that

I needed to write that. I needed because it was so much inside me that I felt I needed to get it out and share it. I felt that my story was a story of self-exploration, and it could help someone else in theirs.

MOMENTS *of*
SUBCONSCIOUS EXCELLENCE,

they only come from
MOMENTS *of*

SILENCE, *or*
RELAXATION, *or*
A COMPLETE INNER FOCUS.

I had a lot of reluctant moments where I wanted to stop and quit writing this book. You can call it procrastination; you can call it fear. It was more of the fear of what other people think or how they will perceive it. However, the deeper I went inside myself through nature walks, gym workouts, on the yoga mat, while journaling or during meditation, the more I felt the need to put it all in a book.

One thing I told myself was that if only one person and one person alone would be impacted by what am I about to write, then this would be enough.

I was on an interview with the famous Ken Walls on his online show "Breakthrough Walls with Ken," where I was asked a specific question regarding why and what stops people from achieving success or probably money, or other things in their lives. This is where I reflected on the fear of not knowing what it means when we become something else or someone else because we change as we grow into our being. We do not know our impact or what it might entail. We prefer to be in our familiar known state. This was one fear I have faced.

FLOW

Flow is the intersection of creativity and productivity, the meeting point of doing and being, the confluence of creative and active. Your life will never work if there's a huge space between who you truly are and the person you are meant to be. If you do not have a space or time to reflect and understand what you want and how you can get there, this means you will always continue to struggle and stay in the rat race and continue on doing without reflecting on being and without allowing ideas to come to you. I don't believe we want to stop doing, but we want to balance the doing and being for us to live a purposeful, meaningful life that we love to live. It is very subjective between each and every person.

FLOW

is the intersection of

creativity & productivity

the meeting point of

doing & being

the confluence of

creative & active

Flow can be experienced in many ways. What works for me is a morning routine that has been embedded to my own style since I read the Robin Sharma's book *The 5:00 AM club*. (R. Sharma, 2018)

I reflect best in the morning. This is what works for me. Some people reflect best before going to bed. Choose what works best for you.

- Meditate.
- Sit in silence.
- Journal.
- Apply breathing techniques.
- Walk in nature.
- Paint.
- Engage in a creative activity.

George Bernard Cho, was asked on his deathbed, "What could you do if you could live your life all over again?" He replied, after a long pause, "I wish I could become the person I know I was meant to be." (Trent Slaney, 2013)

Remember, it is never too late for you to become the person you've always wanted to be.

Start being that person I am talking about, that human being of your dreams.

Reflect, reflect, reflect and reflect. Spend time on reflection.

Another important action you need to take is to cut down energy vampires from your life. These energy vampires could be the distractions that you spend time on that are not serving you. Remember, this will not work if you are not willing to put in some action and commitment towards yourself and your own self-development. Ask yourself today what actions do you do to work on any dimension of your wellbeing?

When you decide on your contentment level in each of the dimensions of wellbeing, it triggers you to start taking action: How do you want to continue, and what do you want change?

The journey starts with BE-ing, being then flows into DO-ing, then again into BE-ing, then into DO-ing. This is the flow of wellbeing. Somewhere (buried deep) within each one of us is a call to purpose. It is not always rational, not always clearly delineated, and sometimes even seemingly absurd. However, the knowing is there.

Dyer (2004) in his book *The Power of Intention* says: "Somewhere, buried deep within each of us, is a call to purpose. It's not always rational, not always clearly delineated, and sometimes even seemingly absurd, but the knowing is there. There's a silent something within that intends you to express yourself. That something is your soul telling you to listen and connect through love, kindness, and receptivity to the power of intention."

The only way we can navigate into a state of being is by developing a level of emotional consciousness. It is a level of developing your self-awareness. It is through the choices you decide to make. Let us assume you have evaluated your dimensions up there. You have to start somewhere. Whether you decided to start an exercise routine, waking up and meditating instead of staying in bed, or changing what you eat. As you make new and better choices, this will help you to come back to balance. You will feel better, I guarantee you. The new choices that you will take will definitely lead you to a change in your emotional state. At the beginning, it'll be very hard. Change is very hard, and you will want to give up. Your body will want to go back to its previous habits, and this is usually called your unconscious state because it's just very natural; it is your comfort zone, you will experience doubt.

Some people around you will tell you, why are you changing? Why do you spend so much time running outside? Why do you spend so much time journaling or meditating? They will criticise you, but it is your own purpose. Embrace this change until you become satisfied with yourself and your choices. As you continue to make the decisions that positively serve your wellbeing, you begin to create a new journey of yourself in all these aspects of your life.

CALL to BE

How do you go into a journey of wellbeing?

- **Write a Not To-Do list.**
  - What are the actions or tasks that you do that does not serve you at all? Get rid of them.
- **Prepare a To-Be list.**
  - It can be meditation, journaling, walking, sitting in silence, mindfulness exercises, breathing exercises etc.
  - Choose what resonates with you from some of the examples I mentioned about reflection above, or maybe do your own research.
- Reflect your level of contentment in each of the below:

Wellbeing Dimension	What is your level of contentment in this dimension?	What actions I want to take to improve this?
Physical		
Emotional		
Spiritual		
Financial		
Social		
Environmental		
Intellectual		

What is the one small thing that you want to begin to change today that will have a positive impact on your life? All of the above could serve you in spending time by reflecting with yourself on what you want to do and how you want to be.

This leads us into the next chapter where we will be deep diving into values and their importance in our lives.

CHAPTER 6

STRUCTURE THE UNSTRUCTURED

VALUES ARE THE DRIVING FORCE BEHIND OUR ACTION

Let us start with a quote from the Dalai Lama: "Open your arms to change, but don't let go of your values." There is so much power in this statement. It confirms to us that, yes, we need to be open to change to be able to elevate ourselves through our lives, but we always need to have a set of principles that guide us while we are doing that.

Allow me to share with you one of my favourite career roles that I've had throughout my life. It was when I was a head of a department. Everything in that department was aligning with me. I was feeling very happy, productive, choosing great people to work with me. I had the best, most amazing boss around me. Simultaneously, the company's values aligned with my own values.

Since the company's values aligned with my values, the results were coming out excellent, and I was able to understand why I was there and how things were coming into fruition with my career. Because of this alignment, I was motivated, engaged, happy to go to work, and every action that I was doing around me in my role reflected this happiness.

On the other hand, I've also faced the opposite situation in a different role, where I was feeling unproductive and disengaged. At that moment, I didn't understand the reason why. I didn't know this would stress me. It was all related to alignment with my vales. Until I went into my coaching journey, I didn't know that the actions of the other people were impacting how I was feeling even though the actions were not directly about me.

Whenever something happens in my life, I always ask myself, "Why does this stress me out? Why does the behaviour of this other person potentially trigger negative emotions in me?" I always come back to the realisation that one of the reasons is because our values are not in alignment. This realization has become like a compass for me, guiding my choices of the people I surround myself with and the actions or decisions I make. It serves as the backbone for everything I do.

Going back to what Dalai Lama says, "Do not let go of your values." Absolutely. We need to carry our values in our heart, and by the end of this chapter, we're going to get very clear on our values, and how we find our values, and how we use them as our framework to evaluate our choices.

Getting clear on what your values are can be very challenging, but knowing what your values are can change your life, for sure. Most of us do not know our personal core values. We are mainly influenced by culture and societal values. And for those of us who are working, we are sometimes influenced by the company values, which is our workplace. Value, provide us with a personal code of conduct, guide or behaviour. Our core values are the framework in which we evaluate our choices.

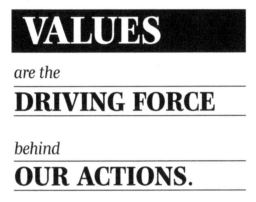

VALUES

are the

DRIVING FORCE

behind

OUR ACTIONS.

ROLE MODELS

Have you ever thought about your values? Do you use them as your guide for the decisions in your life? Have you ever asked yourself what values are guiding you in life or your day-to-day decisions? Take some time to reflect on this, because if you do use them and you have clarity on them, that's a great position at which to start. But if you don't, it is important that you go digging deeper into what your values are. One of the ways that we could look into what our values could be is looking into some of the role models that we've had in our lives. Take a moment and think about somebody who is your role model. What are the qualities of this individual that you admire? What do they entail as core values? And what actions have they made that inspired you?

If you've been, for example, inspired by your grandpa or your grandma, or maybe your boss, or a friend especially when they are being fair, this is a reflection that you hold the value of "Fairness." It means that Fairness is a core value for you because it is something that you've admired in somebody else. Hence, they started to take a place in your life as your role models.

I had a boss in one of my jobs before who was definitely one of my role models when it came to business. That person was very ethical, fun, engaging, transparent, authentic and displayed a high level of integrity as well as the trait of doing the right thing even when no one was watching. He reflected all the qualities of motivating other people, of being a platform for listening to people's issues. That person was quite an inspiration. I wanted to be like him. I've always looked up to that person.

Allow me to share another role model who is a significant part of my family: my mother. I strongly believe that family is where love and life begin. It is where our hearts reside and what brings us joy. My mother embodies the value of kindness, being pleasant, and nurturing to everyone. Personally, I have always admired her kindness and willingness to help others. Therefore, she is one of my role models. It is crucial for us to reflect on the role models in our lives as they truly exemplify the reasons we admire them and why they resonate with our values.

VALUES

Let's go deeper into the understanding of our values. What are values? Values could be seen as individual beliefs, or even fundamental basic beliefs, or moral principles, or accepted standards for a specific person. They determine our priorities in our life. If we go to the verb, to value something means that you need to be able to consider it with respect because you're giving it value. *Values* is kind of the noun of that is the related to the beliefs that motivate us. They are the core backbone of how we move on in our lives. It is the core of us being a human being. Some of them could be inherent values that are specific to ethics, and love, humanity, honesty. Some other values are reflected into the fundamental human beings' values of goodness.

However, there are so many values that we can look at and we can prioritise in our lives. When we don't align with our values, decisions that we take can cause a lot of consequences. We become angry, resentful, frustrated, and then we sometimes do not know why we are feeling those emotions at the specific time.

However, if we are in line with an awareness of what our values are, we are enhancing our lives to the better. Because the moment that you are aligned with your own personal values, it makes it so much easier, and it puts you in a position of high self-awareness that makes you take your decisions as aligned with your values, in a conscious way. Consciously, you take certain decisions, take certain actions, react with certain behaviours as aligned with your own set of values. Once we understand that they are our core principles, we can always ask ourselves, "If I do this today, is it aligning with my values?" If the answer is yes, this means go ahead with it. If the answer is no, ask yourself why it does not align with this value that you hold. Once you understand why it is not aligning, you get a little bit of clarity on what you don't value and why you shouldn't take such a decision.

Some people sometimes will consciously or unconsciously use their core values to choose friendships, relationships, and even business partnerships. This is a very core, how can I say, *backbone*, again. I repeat that it's a core backbone to ensure that we are using our language of values whenever we are aligning ourselves with being more self-aware, because those values act as a moral compass, as we said before. If you know that your values are determined through life and experiences, and now that you are trying to align yourself with your own values, you become more intentional in making your relationships work, in making your work feel more meaningful, in making your life have a better meaning, and you feel more engaged in everything that you're participating in.

One question would that arises is: how do you identify your values? Go back to the exercise where we talk about the role models, and list two or three role models and what values you think they might have. Do they put them on display? If you don't have any role models, maybe write down rewarding or challenging situations that taught you something in your life.

Another way would be to go through a list of values and identify what yours are, from those. A list is shared at the end of this chapter.

Once you look at the list of values that you have identified, ask yourself these questions: Are these values coming very naturally to me? Are they making me feel authentic or aligned? Or do they make me inauthentic, or unaligned or misaligned? And then ask yourself: Out of these values, which ones are the hardest for me to display at times? Once you identify your top values, ask yourself: Are you proud of these values? Do they make you feel good? This is the time for you to reaffirm your values.

From this list of values, ask yourself which values are going to be the ones that you will have in you core every single day. If they are related to ethical values, ask yourself which ones are going to be core ones that will drive your core ethical self? Which ones can drive some positivity in my relationships? Which ones will drive wellbeing and good health in me? Which ones will drive maybe abundance or a better way of living?

What I would recommend you do is you write your set of values down and place it where it's always visible to you. Perhaps your computer at work, it could be in your wallet, it could be in your car, it could be on top of your mirror, it could be on your nightstand; anywhere that you have an opportunity to be visual with your values. You can even write a values statement. For example, if kindness is one of your top values, a value statement would be something to the tune of, "I treat everyone around me with kindness" or "I am a kind person who is respected by family, friends, loved ones and my chosen communities."

Once you have identified your values list and begin to actively align with them, you will notice a significant difference in your life. For instance, during the pandemic, which triggered the authenticity crisis that compelled me to write this book, I experienced a sense of misalignment with certain decisions being made in my workplace. These decisions contradicted my personal values, and despite my efforts to make a positive impact, I felt powerless and unable to effect change. This served as a real-life example of the impact of values alignment or misalignment.

The authenticity crisis I faced led to nights of tears, sadness, frustration, and a strong urge to speak out. I couldn't allow myself to remain silent about certain matters. This crisis became the foundation of my journey towards self-awareness, as it enabled me to recognise and understand my core values. It provided an opportunity for me to fully embrace these values that define who I am. It also heightened my consciousness about my thoughts and emotions, and allowed me to consistently listen to my inner voice, which sometimes says "no" for a reason. When that inner voice is not aligned with my values, there's a purpose behind it.

This journey towards authenticity has given me the chance to lead a more purposeful life, and I now feel that I am honouring the commitments I made to myself. I find fulfillment in pursuing something that truly ignites my soul.

Being aligned with my values and having this authenticity crisis, now I tell myself when I am faced with a misalignment, "Hey, you are being angry because their values and your values don't align. You don't have to agree. You just have to understand that it is not from you. It is the misalignment." This is self-awareness in action.

VALUE-BASED CHOICES

To guide you through this and ensure its effectiveness, you need to be very honest with yourself. It's not enough to simply understand your values because it is not always easy to grasp them. However, you must place significant importance on comprehending the value of this exercise and acknowledge the challenges it presents in understanding your own personal values. For this to work, your personal values need to be the core of who you are and who you want to be. They should guide your choices. You should make choices that are always value-based. You should lean on your values to guide you whenever you have many options around you. If you have a lot of options around you, use the values as your guiding force.

A value-based choice will make your life choices easier in the long run. Once you are aligned with yourself, they will evoke a lot of inspiration in you. Again, they are your driving force behind your behaviours, your actions, your alignment, and your ability to be grounded. Take a lot of time to work on your values, reflect on every action that you do in your life and say, do they represent my values, or they are misaligned with my values?

Remember, as I shared in my story before, when you're feeling something is going wrong, it might mostly be related to some non-value alignment. This is why your resentment, and your dissatisfaction, are amplified in situations where your values are being challenged. Try to reflect on your situations and on the decisions that are around you, and always reaffirm your values and re-look at how they fit in your life. It is highly recommended that every 12 months you revisit your values report or your values exercise listed below, and maybe add to it, and maybe dig deeper into reflecting on them.

Living a value-based life will put you at a position where you take better informed decisions, it makes you feel in alignment and, as this chapter's title says, structured the unstructured. Because you're structuring your life, you're able to understand that you have something to lean on and this is just amazing to be in.

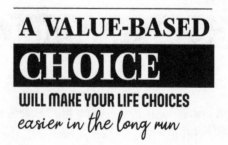

A VALUE-BASED
CHOICE
WILL MAKE YOUR LIFE CHOICES
easier in the long run

CALL *to* VALUES

- From the below set of values, examine some of the more commonly observed life values, and circle the ones that stick out to you or that you believe are a part of who you are as a person.

List of Values

- *Accountability Authenticity Achievement Adaptability Adventure Appreciation Authority Autonomy Balance Beauty Belonging Boldness Care Career Compassion Collaboration Challenge Commitment Community Competency Confidence Connection Contribution Contentment Cooperation Courage Creativity Curiosity Determination Dignity Diversity Empathy Environment Efficiency Equality Ethics Excellence Fairness Faith Fame Family Financial Stability Forgiveness Freedom Friendships Fun Future Generosity Giving back Grace Gratitude Growth Harmony Happiness Health Home Honesty Hope Humility Humour Influence Inclusion Independence Integrity Intelligence Initiative Intuition Joy Justice Kindness Knowledge Leadership Learning Legacy Love Leisure Loyalty Mastery Openness Optimism Order Passion Patriotism Patience Peace Perseverance Pleasure Power Poise Popularity Pride Recognition Reliability Resourcefulness Responsibility Respect Responsibility Reputation Risk-taking Safety Security Self-discipline Selflessness Self-Respect Serenity Service Simplicity Spirituality Stability Success Sustainability Status Talent Teamwork Time Tradition Travel Trust Truthfulness Uniqueness Usefulness Vision Vulnerability Wealth Well-being Wisdom.*

- Take time to determine your most important values based either on the situations that you faced or the people that are your role models.
- Put them on a list in order of most important to least important.
- Once you take that time and look at all the list of values that are very important for you, try to identify at least 10 that resonate with you fully, that you feel that represent who you are or who you want to grow into. You can select less than 10 if you want to.
- These values that you will select need to be intentional and meaningful, aligned with your previous experiences, with your relationships, your role model and with everything that is a representation of you.
- Create value statements as explained before about each of the values you have chosen.
- Keep your values list handy and refer to it when required.

This is a great exercise for you to do, in order to have a representation and a reflection of values in your life.

CHAPTER 7

EUPHORIA

IT'S NOT POSSIBLE TO EXPERIENCE CONSTANT EUPHORIA, BUT IF YOU ARE GRATEFUL, YOU CAN FIND HAPPINESS IN EVERYTHING

I find euphoric moments in learning something new. I call it in my own terms, the euphoria of learning. When was the first time you learned how to ride a bicycle or maybe how to swim? Many of these activities, we learn them as kids, and they become second nature to us.

Finding
EUPHORIC
MOMENTS
in learning something new is
THE EUPHORIA
OF LEARNING.

Well, let me tell you my story with swimming. I was very afraid to go on my front side and I was only able to swim on my back. Yes, that was true. I learned how to swim properly at the age of 39.

Quite a number of years ago, me and my friends went on a trip to Marmaris, Turkey. Over there, you go on the boat trips, and they stop at islands where people can swim a bit, refresh and come back on the boat. The water is so clean and fresh. You can see clearly from the freshness and cleanliness of the water.

So, two of my close friends were both were good at swimming. They would go down from the boat, swim and come back. Some other people were even jumping from the boat. However, I would go down with floaters and, mind you I was in my 30s then, I would watch the people around me. They were swimming calmly. There was nothing that was disturbing them. The whole scene is stuck in my head.

Given the fact that I also have scoliosis, as I mentioned in the previous chapter, swimming was one recommendation that I was given because it helps your spinal cord. I also used to admire those people who did some swimming drills in the swimming pool, going back and forth. They have their swimming gadgets with them.

At the age of 39, I made the decision to enrol in swimming classes. I told Diana, the swimming instructor, that I wanted to learn from scratch. Let me tell you, my coach Diana, to whom I owe a great deal, is one of the best swimming instructors. Our lessons began with submerging under water and counting breaths. Then we progressed to drills and timing to build confidence. To keep it brief, I was determined to attend these classes and diligently practiced all the required drills. I invested my passion, time, and patience into it. I won't claim to be the best swimmer in the world, but I was able to achieve what I desired.

In summer 2022, I went on another trip with a very dear friend of mine to Gocek in Turkey and, with bit of a nudge from my friend, I was able to go out of the boat and swim without floaters. Not only did I go once, but I was able to go down at every stop of the boat and we went on boat trips for three consecutive days. Why am I telling you this story?

The reason is that I want this chapter to enable you to reflect on how the beginner's mindset can help you to explore many possibilities, the impact of feeling empowered and accepting to learn something from scratch. I am not talking about the deliberate practice that has been scientifically proven that if you want to learn something, you need to put it in manageable stages, which is the technique that my swimming instructor applied. It is more just feeling the ability of wanting to learn something new.

NEUROPLASTICITY

What stands between us of learning something new like a skill or a new language is embracing the beginner's mindset. Did you know that the ability for the brain to rewire itself to respond to new challenges is called neuroplasticity?

Neuroplasticity means that our brain is able to modify, change or adapt both our structure and the function throughout our life in response to experiences. Learning a new way to get to a store is neuroplasticity. Creating art or writing is neuroplasticity. Why it is important to know a little bit about neuroplasticity?

We are shifting beliefs and habits. In the chapters before, we spoke about beliefs and habits, about being and doing. There are a lot of biological changes that happen when we overcome some of the conditioning that we've had in our lives. Our nervous system is able to change its activity in response to the changes that we do. Learning a new language is neuroplasticity. Here I am, displaying neuroplasticity by learning how to swim, and I've had that in many things that I learned throughout the years as an adult.

Did you ever think that learning how to swim, or how to create conceptual photography, or how to paint, or how to exercise yoga, may have something in common? Maybe you think they don't, but they do. Going through the few of the skills that I learned as an adult, the process had so much in common even if the skill was different. The common process is like the one I had to go through when I took a course of staged photography. For a staged photo to be created, it starts with inspiration, then the narrative of the story that you want to tell, followed by the direction, and lastly the technique. Let me walk you through the story.

LOVE OF PHOTOGRAPHY

I have always loved photography, and here I am with my new DSLR, having learned its techniques. I no longer need to rely on auto mode for photo shoots. I have become aware of the exposure triangle and the importance of lighting. I understand the elements of a photo, including ISO, shutter speed, and aperture. I am now capable of capturing photos with items in focus, with the background in focus, and with everything in focus. It's just a matter of pressing buttons and adjusting settings, and I feel immensely proud.

Wow, look at me! I started carrying my camera everywhere and practicing all the time. But that wasn't enough.

Strangers or friends were asking me, "What kind of photography do you shoot?"

Me: "I don't know. I am trying to figure it out."

What? I don't know, this was always coming into my head. I don't know what type of photography I like to shoot. I started to explore options and research different types of photography. Then I fell in love with conceptual photography.

I booked a course in Beirut to learn more about conceptual photography.

This is where it all came into perspective. I went into not only how to use the DSLR, but then I went into planning and executing a conceptual photo. You will see below two of the photos that I had taken after the course.

Let me walk you through the process of learning how to take a photo:

- Inspiration: How to come up with the ideas and what is the inspiration process of this idea? In this process, you select what is inspiring you to create. This creative process is like problem-solving.
- Narrative: What is the story you want to tell? Is it an internal or external reflection? What is the intention and the message from the story?
- Direction: In this case, because it's photography, the direction is art direction. This is where we are supposed to be looking at props, colours, locations, wardrobes etc.
- Technique: In this case it refers to the photo taking process like light and the technique that is supposed to be used.

When wanting to learn anything new, I personally do not find it any different from the above process.

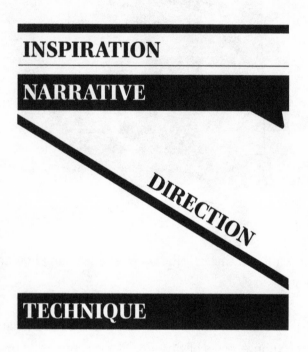

SWIMMING

When I wanted to learn how to swim, the process was the following:

The inspiration was that I wanted to be able to swim on vacation when boats stop on the side. I love seeing people with swimming gear and the fun that they have, and I am motivated to learn from scratch. What was the narrative? What is the story that I was telling myself? It was integrating a new lifestyle. It was being able to practice this sport to my ability and change the status quo of what I know about it. In addition, my narrative was having fun.

As for Direction, I asked, "Where is the best school to learn? What mindset do I have to apply and when do I go?"

Lastly the technique was to learn the basics and practice the technique. The technique was what the instructor has applied during the classes.

I tell you, I learned recently in my master's class, that there is a social comparison theory where we keep on comparing ourselves to the others. In some of my individual swimming classes, a little girl was also learning swimming and she was the next student after me. I was 39 years of age. Can you imagine? However, I was still very motivated as I had a narrative in my head.

I had a new story that I wanted to tell myself. I had an inspiration that was there. Also, I hired one of the best swimming instructors. She was teaching me the techniques from scratch. I was willing to learn the basics. We learned the breathing techniques. We had to go under the water and count to 10 or count to 10-Mississippi. (For those who watch Friends, there is an episode that speaks about that).

Am I a perfect swimmer today? No. But do I know how to swim? Yes. Do I worry about swimming in deep water? Absolutely, I still do. Do I prefer that the swimming pool is of a depth where I am able to sometimes stand on my feet? 100%. Do I breathe perfectly? Maybe not. But I still learnt the technique. This in itself is progress.

YOGA

When it is hard and you are demotivated, go back to step number one. What inspired you? Remember the story that you are telling yourself. The same thing happened with me when I was going to yoga. I've done some yoga classes in the past, but a close friend of mine also took me to a yoga class where many of the movements in the yoga practice I didn't know, but I was still not comparing myself.

On a yoga mat, being present is key and not comparing yourself to anyone else is part of the experience. It's your own practice. It has embedded this beginner's mindset in me even more because I was only progressing based on my personal ability. There were days where I was not able to even stand in the positions. Yoga has helped me to accept the fact that where I am today is where I am *present*. This was also helping me with what stories I tell myself and how these might or might not be serving me.

PAINTING

A friend of mine has taken me to a painting class as a gift for my birthday, given that I love photography and art. I was going through my self-awareness journey and when learning how to paint, I was being very meticulous in making sure that everything was very much in alignment, and perfect and structured.

Over there, what story was I telling myself? What was the inspiration? My narrative was letting go and being more creative. I started to go to dine-and-art style events where we learn how to paint in an engaging environment with light snacks and music. Then, lesson after lesson, painting after painting, it started to flow in me. The direction I was aiming for was that this was my time for me to be creative, and to learn from scratch.

EGOLESS LEARNING

Why am I sharing my stories with you? Because you could be at this moment wanting to learn something new and you are worried about people's opinions. You might be worried about things like where you stand at that level. Trust me, you would be surprised. No one cares. And then when you do it, they tell you, "When do you find the time to do it?"

A few of the things that are important when wanting to be or to act like a beginner is to be inspired from children. They are playful. They display playfulness with the beginner's mindset at all times. Remember that you want to practice progress and not perfection. Put your ego on the side and be open for mistakes. I call it egoless learning. Learning by trial and error. You're only learning and not performing.

EGOLESS LEARNING:
PUT YOUR EGO ON THE SIDE, *and*

BE OPEN FOR MISTAKES.

Remember that experimentation is very important. If you don't do it and you don't know how it is being done, how do you know where you stand in it? What is your level? Slow down and celebrate every step on the way. No matter what happens to you on the path of learning, keep on going. That is my recommendation.

SLOW DOWN *and*
CELEBRATE
every step on the way.

Keep going has many meanings: persevere with, perpetuate, continue with, internalise, persist with, go on with.

KEEP GOING:

PERSEVERE WITH,
PERPETUATE,
CONTINUE WITH,
INTERNALISE,
PERSIST WITH,
GO ON WITH.

No matter how hard it is, just keep going because you will only fail when you give up. In learning something new, there is no failure. It is the permission that you give yourself not to be perfect at something. Enjoy the process and every step on the way. Share what you learn. The best way to keep learning any practice is sharing what you learn with somebody who you feel it can benefit from it. Knowledge increases your level of learning.

GIVE YOURSELF
PERMISSION
NOT TO BE PERFECT
at something.

Long ago there was a Zen master. This Zen master was very wise, and people came from all across the land to be instructed in the art of Zen. One day, a successful and important man came to the Zen master and he said, "I have come to learn the art of Zen. Please teach me your wisdom." "Very well," said the Zen master. "Before we begin, let me make us a pot of tea."

The Zen master put on the teapot, brewed the tea and brought out two cups. He began to pour the tea into the successful man's cup, but he didn't stop when the cup was full. He continued to pour. And the tea spilled over the sides and all over the table. "Stop," the successful man said. "Can't you see that the cup is full? What are you doing?" "You are like this teacup," the Zen master answered. "You are already full of knowledge. There is no room for anything else. I cannot teach you anything until you come to me with an empty mind."

Unlearning and Relearning

This is where I recommend unlearning and relearning. When I went back to my swimming, I told her, "Teach me from scratch. I don't want to be influenced by anything that I knew from the past." I tell you, the unlearning process is quite hard because we've spoken in the past about our beliefs. We've spoken about our habits. There needs to be a progression in the way that we want to do things because if you have been doing something for a period of time, you have developed it as a habit.

Now, unless you consciously unlearn what you have learned by applying the mindset, by wanting to do things in a completely different way, by accepting that you are learning, by accepting that you could be failing, by accepting that it's only progress, that is the only way that you will be able to learn and progress. For this to work, you need to have a beginner's mindset. You need to unlearn and relearn.

Again, I repeat to you the importance of having a beginner's mindset because it is just like kids who have a sense of wonder, who are connected to egoless learning and who are looking at what inspires them. They just have fun. They always unlearn and relearn all the time. What is the skill you have been postponing to learn? And why have you been postponing it? What story are you telling yourself? And what are you going to do that you have learned the beginner's mindset now and the steps of learning a new skill?

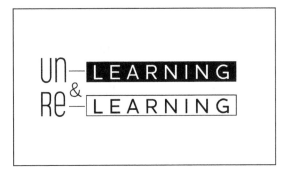

Treat everything that you want to learn like a road of creativity. It is the art piece, which is you. Julia Cameron, the author of The Artist's Way, a book for inspiring creativity in your life, once said, "No matter what your age or your life path, whether making art is your career or your hobby or your dream, it is not too late or too egotistical or too selfish or too silly to work on your creativity."

I am not telling you go for photography classes, painting classes or anything that I mentioned above. All I'm telling you is that it could be you going to ride a bicycle, maybe learn a new language or anything you've always wanted to learn, maybe an action from your TO-BE list. I encourage to take the first step.

CALL *to* EUPHORIA

- List 3 things you wished you learned, or you wanted to improve on.
- For each one of them, fill in the below:
  - Inspiration: What is your inspiration? What is your Why?
  - Narrative: What is the story you want to tell and what is the intention behind that story?
  - Direction: What is the direction you want to take to learn it? What mindset do you want to apply through the process?
  - Technique: What technique best fits your learning?
- For each of the three things you mentioned above, write down what you want to *unlearn* in relation to the subject, and what do you prefer to *relearn*.

This leads us to one of the activities that I personally have enjoyed most in my lifetime, which is travelling. You might wonder why it has its chapter of its own. It's because it plays a hugely important part in my life and I'm going to share a few of my travel stories in the next chapter.

IF YOU ARE
GRATEFUL,
YOU CAN FIND

HAPPINESS

in everything.

CHAPTER 8

CARPE DIEM

IT'S THAT NUMINOUS MOMENT WHERE YOU FEEL IN AWE OF LIFE

Wanderlust is a very popular word you must have heard in many of the social media channels or traveller's blogs. It is something that is all over the place. It is defined as a strong desire to travel. For me, it means so much more than that. It is more than a passion or lust. It's a feeling, it's an emotion, it's a lust not only to explore the world, but more to explore myself. My deepest passions, my desires, my ability to see the world with new set of eyes have all been revealed when I was somewhere around the world. No one has ever been hurt from jet lag. That's the spirit that feeds my desire. While travelling, whether it's getting lost across a hidden backstreet, an old café, trying authentic food, or connecting with a local, it's always a chance to encounter a magic moment. I am always in a carpe diem state of mind when I am on a trip, exploring a new place. For me, this is storytelling at its best. This is where stories give life to life.

A CARPE DIEM
STATE OF MIND
on a trip.
EXPLORING A NEW PLACE.

By the end of this chapter, we will reflect on how travel impacts us. We will see how travel reflects my own humanity, how it has triggered my own creativity, how it opened my mind to new connections and how it helped me evolve and how I learned to stay connected. We were taught that we are not allowed to speak to strangers. However, meeting people from around the world has been one of the best expansions of human nature for me. Receiving texts from friends I met during my trips, could this be more rewarding? Could it be more human? In all areas of our lives, we create boundaries. Boundaries, boundaries, boundaries. However, when wanderlust hits, your mind opens up like a flower to the world around it. Anything becomes your everything as you start to display a sense of awe and exploration, flexibility, and practicing the art of being a free soul. It does promote happiness, it opens your heart.

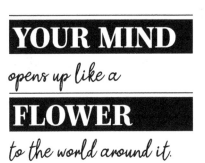

WHEN
WANDERLUST
hits,

YOUR MIND
opens up like a

FLOWER
to the world around it.

The habitual closed mindedness that we are accustomed to, and that we have acquired throughout the years, is replaced by an open mindedness and a cultural engagement when we are on our trips somewhere. Have you ever heard about (*A Quote by Miriam Adeney*, n.d.) which says, "You will never be completely at home again because part of your heart always will be elsewhere. That is the price you pay for the richness of loving and knowing people in more than one place." This is exactly how I feel. Travelling is not only about taking time off from your work, your routine, or the current events that are running in your life. It is much more than that. It is indeed enhancing your own wellbeing in many different ways.

Anything becomes your

EVERYTHING

as you start to display a sense of
AWE *and* **EXPLORATION,**
FLEXIBILITY, *and*
PRACTICING THE ART OF BEING A FREE SOUL.

By being exposed to new places, smells, tastes, sites, locations, we are having new reward circuits reactivated on our brains. Did you know that? This automatically impacts something that is called cognitive flexibility. Cognitive flexibility is defined as the ability to switch one's thinking, which is cognition or a train of thought, as an adaptation to the demand of stimuli. In neuroscience, the term is sometimes referred to as attention switching, cognitive switching, mental flexibility, set shifting, and task switching. It is all about your brain's ability to adapt to new, changing, or unplanned events. It is an indicator of an agile and flexible mind. Having an agile and a flexible mind will enable us to grow these connections in ourselves, and it will also help us to be impacted by greater results.

Travel impacts a lot of areas in our life. It impacts our creativity through enriched experiences that we currently have. Once we travel, we are exposed to various things around us that are probably new to us. Being exposed to this creative aspect in our life will make us become more innovative in the way that we see things, in the way that we look at things. It also helps us to improve our social anxiety. It is proven that when we travel and we are open to connections with different people, we then are more adaptable in our desire to speak to others, and then we are socially comfortable because there is no judgment. We start to think that these people will not judge us, it's the first time that we see them, and then we are socially calmer about it.

TRAVELING

is

STORYTELLING

at its best,

where

STORIES GIVE LIFE *to* LIFE.

The planning part before you travel gives you a sense of happiness. Imagine yourself, you're booking a trip. The research starts, you start to look at different things that you want to do. What is this country famous for? There is this level of positive excitement that starts to well up in you, and then you have this thing that I call, in between parentheses, "the looking forwardness to." And this automatically gives you a high level of happiness. When you are travelling, you are exposed to a lot of emotions, and one of them is the impact of kindness and empathy on you. Because you're going to be seeing people from all around the world, you are not only going to be kind to others, you will also develop a level of flexibility and adaptability. There's a high level of kindness and empathy during your trips, right?

Let's not forget your mindfulness because you're going to be more open minded, you're going to be more educative to your enriched experiences. You will be able to explore new things with a different set of eyes and what was previously something very rigid in your mind may become acceptable when you are travelling. Let us not forget, as well, the stress relief that you receive or you feel when you are away in a new place, because you will be practicing a set of emotions that are breaking the patterns of your daily routine. Because you're breaking the patterns of your daily routines, you are going into a state of "I don't have to be very fast paced at this specific moment. I am going to see new places. My mind is calmer, I'm more peaceful in the way that I am travelling." There are no events to run, you're at your own pace, automatically your stress gets relieved.

For me, I also believe that travel makes you more grateful, because when you are travelling, you are evaluating all the good things that you currently have in your life and all the beauty that is around you. You are gracefully looking at life with a set of eyes that are grateful to all the beautiful things that we see when we are in a new place. We all know that gratitude has a huge impact on our mental and physical health. While travelling, you can choose certain travelling experiences that are very educational that give you a sense of responsibility and could possibly be giving back to the community because they could be something that you either wanted to learn or something that makes you want to give back to the community, or teach other people. You probably want to volunteer in any experience that could be somewhere around the world where you are travelling.

Travelling definitely is very inspirational. It makes you healthier. It relieves your stress, it enhances your creativity, it boosts your happiness and satisfaction, it lowers your risk of stress. At the same time, it is fun. It is a lot of fun because you are exploring new areas, new places. You are outside of your personal environment. You are looking at the beauty of nature. You might be exposed to situations during your journey that can reflect on your purpose or what you always wanted to be aligned with. You are going to meet a lot of new people who are going to definitely add to the stories of wisdom that you've carried around the world. Travelling is always very beneficial.

MY DEEPEST PASSIONS,

MY DESIRES,

MY ABILITY
TO SEE THE WORLD
with new set of eyes

HAVE ALL BEEN REVEALED
when I was somewhere around the world.

Let me share with you some of my personal stories from around the world during my trips. It has played a very important part in my life.

BARCELONA

Let me start with my visit to Barcelona where I was assigned to be on a work-related assignment in a hotel. Over there, I had to stay for almost a month. When I was in Barcelona, and for those who know me very well, they know that I love to watch football and I support Spanish Barcelona team. But that is a completely different story here. When I used to go to the staff restaurant to eat in that hotel, there was an older lady who was working in that restaurant. Through our interactions together, with the little Spanish that I was starting to speak because I was learning it, and with her Spanish, we used to have short conversations about her, about her kids, and about her work and how she loves to be working, and her smile was just out of this world. I remember that this lady became very close to me and whenever I went to the restaurant, she would come and make sure that my food was well taken care of and displayed kindness as well as engaged in storytelling.

On the last week when I was leaving, she came to me with a bracelet that was handmade with beads. There were two. One from her and one from her daughter. They made for me two bead bracelets that I still have with me. And imagine, this lady just felt a level of connection from our conversations, and so much friendship, that she, throughout my lunch breaks, developed a relationship that became significant enough to give me a farewell gift for my visits. It was something that was handmade by her daughter and by her, which are items that they usually sell. I think this is human connections at its best.

AUSTRIA

Let's move now to Austria. Here I am arriving to Vienna from Dubai, and I landed in Vienna because I wanted to visit a friend of mine who had worked with me, and I promised that I would visit her there. I arrived in Vienna and I was walking around the opera house and all these other places and being exposed to everything that was there, the beauty of the city and the culture and the history that was around us. A few days after we arrived in Vienna, we decided that we would go to different cities, and here we were suddenly in the middle of Salzburg. For those who know Salzburg, The Sound of Music movie was filmed there. If you want to go on a trip where you feel that you're out of this world, Salzburg is the place. It's one of the most beautiful places I've ever visited.

While walking with my friend, I noticed all these people wearing *dirndls*, which is a dress traditionally worn by women and girls in Austria, Bavaria and some other countries. I have seen this type of dress before.

I told my friend, "If you ever get married in Salzburg, I promise I will come and attend your wedding." The years went by, and there I was, booking another flight ticket to Vienna and arriving in Vienna to take a train to Salzburg because she was getting married there. Many people from around the world flew to Salzburg to celebrate their wedding. That wedding was incredibly special because I had the opportunity to meet many amazing and wonderful people. Among them, one person became a dear friend of mine, and we ended up visiting each other in the US and going on a wine trip with some other friends. It was one connection leading to another.

While I was in Salzburg, I took a trip on one of the lakes, immersing myself in the breathtaking scenery of mountains and nature, as you can see in the pictures below. It was the most serene and peaceful setting I had ever experienced. Not only did I have the chance to meet new people, but I also connected deeply with nature. I felt like a part of the culture, gaining insight into their wedding traditions, music, and different customs. It was an eye-opening experience that broadened my understanding of how people live around the world. This journey was deeply personal to me.

NEPAL

Nepal has a very special place in my heart because when I arrived there, I didn't know what to expect. I was going on just a little break to explore and see the city. But the kindness of the people and the way that they help and support whoever is asking for anything has been so special to me, and it has been something that is forever in my heart. That was in 2015 before the earthquake took place there. I was taking my camera everywhere and I managed to take a huge set of photos reflecting facial expressions of the people there. In the pictures you see below, they have faces that are with wrinkles, they are aging gracefully, they have a lot of stories expressed through their eyes. The eyes of the people in Nepal tell me a lot of emotional stories. I felt a close human connection to the people whilst taking the photos. I felt a sense of humanity.

HOST FAMILY IN SPAIN

A couple of years ago, I decided to learn a new language, Spanish, because I admired the music and I've always wanted to learn Spanish as a language. I registered in a school in Dubai, and I attended regularly. But during that time, I decided to make a vision board. And on my vision board, I placed one of the things that I wanted to do, which was to travel to a Spanish school and take a course. To cut the story short, the time had come, I did my research and I decided to revisit Malaga. I had visited it before, but I decided to revisit and study Spanish in November 2018.

And during my time there, I asked the school about the different options they provided. One of the options was to live with a host family. So here I am, arriving at the house of this family, who were strangers to me at the time. The school driver picked me up, and the lady of the house was waiting for me. The house was very close to the sea, just a five-minute walk away. Since it wasn't the student season, I had the lower floor all to myself. I had my own bedroom, bathroom, living area, dining table, and a small kitchenette. But I wanted to experience their way of life, so I also signed up to eat with the family.

The family consisted of the husband, the wife, and two teenagers, a boy and a girl. There was another girl from Italy staying on the floor above us, doing an internship at a local company. Suddenly, I found myself living in a stranger's house. I would come home from school, go upstairs, and have dinner with the lady of the house. She taught me how to make eggs with potatoes and introduced me to Spanish cuisine. It's worth noting that they didn't speak English, except maybe the husband to some extent, but not fluently. Yet there I was, living with them for almost a week or maybe a little longer. I studied, took my books to a coffee shop, and returned to the host family. They would check up on me. I spent my evenings with them, practicing the language and truly becoming a part of their family. I learned about their culture, listened to their stories, and discovered how they met, started their family, pursued their education, and so on.

Nobody could convince me that this wasn't a cultural exchange. It was the epitome of humanity at its best. I remember it was close to Christmas season, by then I had become friends with the Italian girl. Even till this day, we still exchange messages, and we plan to meet as we promised. She might visit Dubai soon with her family. I also attended the Christmas tree lighting event in the city of Malaga, which is renowned as one of the top 10 Christmas lighting events in Europe. It was an incredibly beautiful experience. I can still recall the wonderful music. When it was time for me to leave, I made sure to give small Christmas gifts and souvenirs for the family. As I departed from their house, I couldn't hold back my tears. I texted my sister, who reassured me by saying, "You will always come back." It was an emotional moment, similar to the feeling I have when I leave my own family to return to Beirut or elsewhere.

This is not an easy experience. It's not just about visiting people and then leaving. We connect with people. In her book *Eat Pray Love*, Gilbert (2007) emphasises the importance of taking care of our families wherever we find them. Human connection is real, and embracing other cultures is real. It broadens our minds, brings us cultural happiness, and allows us to learn new things. We become more accepting of different aspects of various cultures. It's a beautiful and profound emotion. And to this day, I promise myself that I will meet them again someday. I still exchange texts with my host family. I still feel connected to them. They opened their home to me, regardless of whether it was part of the program or not. Their kindness, empathy, and warm welcome have left a lasting impact on my life. It means a great deal to me.

TUSCANY

Tuscany has one of the closest connections to my heart as well. I love Tuscany because Tuscany loves me. This is what I feel. When I go to Tuscany, the energy level of emotions is amplified. I have this connection with nature. The first day I landed in Tuscany was when I went on a road trip with one of my best friends, and then we wanted to do a full wine tour around different wineries that we loved, and it was like a miracle. I arrived in Tuscany and was staying in this *agriturismo* house, which is a farmhouse in the midst of beautiful greenery. When I look outside the window it's all green and it feels like home. I'm like, "This is home for the next week. Oh, my God, I cannot believe it." The first day I arrived, I was already thinking about the day that I would have to leave and how sad I would feel.

My connection to Tuscany is so deep that I've had many of my beautiful, euphoric emotions with Tuscany. I remember standing on top of a mountain that was just fresh, clean, full of butterflies, and the wind was playing on my face, and I had those euphoric emotions that are beautiful. Carpe diem, seize the moment, and it was indeed a seize the moment for me. The host of that *agriturismo* was very welcoming. We've had a lot of home-cooked cookies and everything else. But at the same time, Italy by itself and the cities and the medieval cities that we visited were just beautiful and so much culture abounds that it makes you feel that you're going back in time and probably looking at places holding historical memories. People from different cultures used to live there. They used to create their music there. They used to paint their portraits, or paint their paintings there. The places had many untold stories.

Tuscany, when you're walking in those streets, you feel strong emotions. I mean, standing in the middle of Siena by itself is a big emotion. You are there and there is a lot of energy. There is a lot of energy of connection to culture and to the place by itself. The food, the people, their attitude towards life, their laid-back nature, the way that they carry themselves, they reflect happiness. You feel that they're having fun and their connection to each other is contagious. For me, it's one of my favourite places in the world.

As I mentioned before, there are many cities I have visited, and the list goes on. For me, these places have always been my go-to destinations. Whenever I felt the need to reflect, connect with others, or reconnect with myself and simply have fun, I would eagerly anticipate booking a trip, even if it was just for two, three, or four days. I feel a sense of belonging in these places. It's not just one place in the world that I identify with; it's more than that. I've visited numerous other countries, and I've only listed a few of them here. Rest assured, when I mentor my team, I always encourage them to make their dream trip a reality. I have several examples from my career where, during mentoring sessions, I pushed team members to step out of their comfort zones and embark on a journey. Two of them took my advice. One went to New York, and another travelled to Asia. When they returned, they were revitalised, more connected, and fully in tune with their true selves. It was a beautiful and profound experience for them.

The memories we create while traveling stay with us for a lifetime. They help shape our true selves, ignite our purpose, and remind us of the value of our interconnectedness. They broaden our perspectives and make us fall in love with the richness of life's offerings. If you don't ask yourself now about your upcoming dream trip, you won't be able to experience its benefits. Shift your focus from material possessions to enriching experiences. That's my heartfelt recommendation. Take the time today to consider booking a trip. It can be a local or international adventure, as long as it promises lots of fun. Don't forget to capture those joyful moments through photographs. Travel teaches us, as human beings, that we share more similarities than we might have thought. Despite our differences in religion, culture, or economic backgrounds, we are connected in meaningful ways.

VISION BOARD

Vision boards are very well-known to be something that is powerful, that allows you to reflect and re-look into things that you are trying to achieve in your life. The moment that you start to put it out in pictures, your mind starts to work on it, and it is there in your subconscious because you're seeing it all the time, and then it starts to open solutions in your head on how you can achieve it.

From a set of magazines or pictures from the internet, vision boards are usually made by cutting the pictures, quotes and other dreams and placing them as a collage on a board.

CALL *to* ADVENTURE

Whatever the reason is, there is something about travel that changes us forever. Let us work together now and create your vision board trip and plan to book it.

- Ask yourself:
  - What is the trip that you always wanted to do, and why is it important to you?
  - What is holding you back?
  - What are the alternative situations to get over the things that are holding you back?
  - What are the best strategies or ideas to immediately act upon in order to capitalise on your full plan?
- Now that you have answered all these questions, I recommend that you either pick up a travel magazine, maybe one or two or three, or go on the internet and find quotes and pictures of places that you want to visit.
- After collecting, cut them and come up with a full list of pictures that you would like your dream trip to look like.
- Once you have cut the photos, start to create your vision board on a piece of cardboard.
- Glue them there and put them in a place where it's in front of you at all times.
- Now plan that trip.

This leads us now, especially given the question we've posed about holding you back, to go into something that I call your inner dialogue.

CHAPTER 9

INNER DIALOGUE

YOU ARE YOUR OWN SUPERHERO. YOUR WORTHINESS IS YOUR POWER

Let's look into this quote by Louise Hay. "You've been criticizing yourself for years and it hasn't worked. Try approving of yourself and see what happens." (L. Hay, 1995)

Yes, you; you, the one reading now; you, you, you, I am talking to you. How many times have you allowed yourself to be judgmental towards yourself? This is different to what we spoke about before in our limiting beliefs and what we would have believed about ourselves throughout the years. This is when you have done your limiting beliefs work and now you are not prioritising kindness towards your beautiful self. How many times have you called yourself names? How many times have you used terms like, "I should have, I shouldn't have," etc? How many times have you ignored your own intuition and blamed yourself for it? By the end of this chapter, we will have dived into self-care, through self-compassion and self-love.

you are
YOUR OWN
SUPERHERO.

YOUR WORTHINESS *is*
YOUR POWER.

SELF-COMPASSION

What is self-compassion? The definition of self-compassion entails being warm and understanding towards ourselves when we suffer, fail or feel inadequate, rather than ignoring our pain or flagellating ourselves with self-criticism.

Why self-compassion? Because it is associated with wellbeing, and this book is written as an exploration of the journey of the self. This is a huge, big part of it.

My personal story with self-compassion includes the fact that I have always held myself accountable and resilient towards achievement. When I was writing this book, I was reluctant at certain times, and I stopped for a few months from writing anything related to this book because I was being very self-judgemental. I was asking myself, "Who would read it, and why would they read it?" I was the first person to criticise myself. They usually call it self-critique. Many of the ideas were coming to my head and were like, "Why do you want to write this book? Who do you think you are? Why is it important for you to write it? I don't think you are smart enough to do that." These were some of the ideas and questions that were coming up in my mind regarding me writing the book. I faced an imposter syndrome about writing.

For those of you who do not know what an imposter syndrome means, it is doubting our abilities and feelings even in areas in which we normally excel. Because I was finding it a little bit difficult to have this message that I want to put out in the world, the only time that I was able to get through the book and now having you read it, is when I leaned on self-compassion and when I allowed myself to be compassionate with myself. I told myself, "If only one person will benefit from me writing a book, I need to write it because it is aligning with my personal purpose."

IF ONLY ONE PERSON
will benefit from me
writing a book,
I need to write it
because it is aligning with
MY PERSONAL PURPOSE.

Self-compassion is a real thing. It is something that we need to always lean on and have in our lives. We're not talking about self-love and self-compassion in the form of it being, for example, something that is selfish. We're talking about it as an attitude towards ourselves.

LEAN *on*
SELF-COMPASSION.

SELF-COMPASSION TO WELLBEING

Self-compassion is a kind of attitude towards ourselves, rather than beating ourselves up or putting ourselves in painful moments. Even when we are in painful moments, rather than displaying harsh self-criticism on ourselves, or maybe saying words that are self-degrading to ourselves, compassion is a big thing to display towards ourselves. This doesn't mean we avoid the pain, but we embrace it with more kindness and goodwill.

By offering oneself kindness and understanding, we can reduce feelings of shame, self-blame, and self-criticism. This, in turn, promotes greater emotional stability, self-acceptance, and overall psychological well-being.

By practicing self-compassion, we develop a growth mind-set and embrace the learning opportunities within failures or setbacks. This supports our overall psychological and emotional health, leading us to improved wellbeing.

SELF-LOVE

If you look at the stories from Louise Hay, it is clear that she has a lot of stories to share about self-love and also known as one of the founders of the self-help movement. She worked on a lot of affirmations on what we tell ourselves. Millions of people have learnt how to manifest more of what they want in their lives, including greater wellbeing in their bodies, minds, and spirits, thanks to Louise's healing methods and positive attitude. (*About Louise Hay | Bio & Timeline of Achievements*, 2022)

How do we ensure that we tell ourselves the right things? Louise Hay says that if we are willing to do the mental work, almost anything can be healed in ourselves. (L. Hay, 1995)

She says that: "Loving ourselves is about being kind to ourselves." She encourages everybody to stop scaring themselves, to be gentle with themselves, to be kind and patient with themselves, to love their negatives, to take care of their body. These are many of the aspects of self-love highlighted by Louise Hay. (L. Hay, 1995)

With positive affirmations, you cultivate wholesome thoughts and concepts that help you grow in self-esteem and confidence as well as in finding inner pleasure and tranquillity. They are for different topics like health, happiness, healing, abundance, self-esteem and much more. Affirmations said aloud are the most effective.

Some positive affirmations suggested are:

- Wellness is a natural state of my body.
- I am active and alive.

- I am surrounded by love.
- Abundance flows freely through me.
- I am a unique beautiful soul.

You have nothing to prove to anybody. If you were your own best friend, how would you treat your own self? Display a high level of self-awareness and self-acceptance? When you make a mistake, do not beat yourself up. "I should have done it, or I should have done that." Instead, re-look at why you have taken the decision and allow yourself to say to yourself that, "I did it with the level of mind that I currently have. I thought it was the best solution."

WHEN YOU MAKE A
MISTAKE,
DO NOT BEAT YOURSELF UP

"I should have done this,
or
I should have done that."

Be very mindful in ensuring that you are allowing yourself to have this release moment, your inner critique that is in your subconscious.

MINDFULNESS
Practicing mindfulness is also a very good way for you to be in moments with yourself where you're centring yourself.

I recommend yoga or deep breathing, or nature walks at any time.

Recommended are guided meditations that include body scans and also self-compassion breaks.

REFRAMING

Another important aspect of cultivating self-compassion in your life is gaining perspective on certain situations. To achieve this, it's crucial to reframe and consider the bigger picture. I often use a personal example to gain perspective: I imagine myself as a fly on the wall observing my own actions. I do so without judgment or emotional attachment. Through this objective observation, I begin to recognise that some of the things I've said to myself might have been harsh.

Avoid rushing to judgment about yourself. When you find thoughts like "I always do this" or "I always feel that," it's important not to immediately label yourself based on those emotions. While it may differ from limiting beliefs, passing judgments on your emotions puts you in a position where your negative mindset is influencing your positive mindset.

SELF-COMPASSION MANTRA

Another way to work on your own self-compassion is to have a self-compassion mantra. What is a self-compassion mantra? It's a statement or a collection of statements that you tell yourself as a list of affirmations that you can practice. You can list a set and always tell them to yourself. They could be a list of ten or fifteen. Some examples are:

- I am human and I learn from my life experiences.
- I am enough here and now.
- I deserve to forgive myself.
- Shame and self-doubt don't serve me.

SELF-COMPASSION LETTERS

The tools that I usually use when I am wanting to practice self-compassion with myself is writing my self-compassion letters. Writing my self-compassion letters is an important way of expressing to myself how I feel about that specific moment, and also avoiding the self-judgment and allowing myself to be at forgiveness with myself.

JOURNAL PROMPTING

Journal prompting is also a tool that I find effective. It enables people to suffer less, while also helping them to thrive. In your journal and prompted by the list below, write down and reflect what you feel, or you want to express:

- Make a list of 10 ways you can be more understanding and kind to yourself.
- Write about a moment when you failed at something and what you learned as a result of that experience.
- Imagine you are your own best friend and write down how you can support yourself more effectively.
- Write about the things that make you fearful and nervous, as well as the reasons behind your feelings.

- Write about a time when you overcame fear and shown courage and confidence. What gave you that feeling?
- List 10 things you love the most about yourself.

Remember, for this to work, and for you to display self-compassion and getting in tune with your own self-love, you are required to embrace more of who you are and accept the way that you are. Give time to the tools that I've displayed above and be true to your own self.

EMBRACE
who you are!

"You're going to realise it one day, that happiness was never about your job or your degree or being in a relationship. Happiness was never about following in the footsteps of all those who came before you. It was never about being like the others. One day, you're going to see it, that happiness was always about the discovery, the hope, the listening to your heart and following it wherever it chose to go. Happiness was always about being kinder to yourself. It was always about embracing the person you are becoming. One day, you will understand that happiness was always about learning how to live with yourself, that happiness was never in the hands of other people. It was always about you. It was always about you." (Sparacino, 2018)

FOR YOUR
WELLBEING,
lean on

ON SELF-COMPASSION,
practice

MINDFULNESS,
reframe

PERSPECTIVES,

JOURNAL.

GET IN TUNE WITH
YOUR OWN
SELF-LOVE.

As we have said, being very compassionate to ourselves will always allow us to be more positive. It will give us an opportunity to be acceptable to ourselves. It will give us an opportunity to tune better into our emotions. It will make us more self-aware. It will make us be more kind. It will make us more mindful, and it will allow us to thrive and use more positive emotions towards ourselves. This automatically leads me into the next chapter, which will look at how leading ourselves and our inner dimension is intuitive.

CALL *to* SELF-COMPASSION

- Buy yourself a journal to get the work done.
- Choose at least two of the below techniques mentioned in this chapter and commit to practicing them.
- If you choose self-love practice, write down at least 9 affirmations for 9 days showing self-love.
- If you choose Mindfulness, you may choose to either start to practice yoga, or deep breathing or go on a nature walk.
- If you choose Reframing, choose a situation you are facing and then look at it from a different perspective then analyse it as if you are not in it. Change the perspective and then see what happens.
- If you choose self-compassion mantra, write down at least nine mantras, place them in areas where you can see them and read them every day for 3 months.
- If you choose self-compassion letters, commit to writing yourself at least three letters a month for next three months.
- If you choose journal prompting, choose at least three of the above prompts and intend to journal about them in next three months.

"If you want others to be happy, practice compassion.
If you want to be happy, practice compassion."
— Dalai Lama.

This leads us to our inner dimension and intuition.

CHAPTER 10

MASTERING YOUR INNER DIMENSION

SELF-LEADERSHIP IS INTUITIVE

How many times have you felt you were about to take the right decision because your gut feeling was telling you that, but you ended up analysing too much and this led to a different decision? How many times you did take the right decision following your intuition, and then accordingly, you were feeling that you did the right thing?

Talking about intuition allows us to go back to whether intuition is trustworthy in the way that we address things, whether it opens up our lives to more possibilities. Does it sharpen our cognitive sensors and encourages us to take the right decisions? Because at the end of the day, intuition is following our gut feeling.

WHAT IS INTUITION?

Intuition by definition is having the ability to understand or know something without direct evidence or a reasoning process. It is a sense of knowing. It is taking the decision or feeling that this is the right course of action. It is something that you cannot explain. You just say, "It just felt right."

"There is something that is making me feel tuned in or maybe understanding that it might not be rational, but this is where my gut feeling is all about." We know that intuition has helped us many times in the past and where we go back and remember the times where many things that we wanted to take a decision about, we followed our intuition and then it helped us to understand.

Maybe not immediately, but at a period of time in the future, we kind of understood that the decision I took was probably the right one. Then, eventually after some time, many factors present themselves and showcase that listening to our intuition was the right thing to do. Sometimes we tap into our intuition without having the right amount of information, or resources or analysis.

Albert Einstein says that, "The intuitive mind is a sacred gift, and the rational mind is a faithful servant. We have created a society that honours the servant and has forgotten the gift."

I was called one time about a job in a company that I was always interested in. I went through the process, and all was going on very well, but there was something inside me telling me that I shouldn't go for that job. However, everything else around it was rationalising the fact that this is all I wanted to do for the past year. I'd been preparing myself for something like that and started to question why I felt that I did not want to take that decision. My mind was trying to convince me that this was the right thing to do, and I was going through a formal process with the fear of missing out. At the end, something didn't feel right and then I just said to myself that I cannot, I do not want to do that.

A year after, it all made sense: that quick and efficient decision, and listening to my insight, thoughtful reflection, and listening to my heart or gut instead of listening to my head, has led me down the right path to where I wanted to be. It manifested itself for several reasons: I found a better opportunity, and the company I was with had internal issues.

CONSEQUENCES AND INTUITION

How many times have you gone against your intuition, only to experience unfavourable consequences? I'm not suggesting that we shouldn't be rational. It's important to consider different perspectives when following our intuition. However, it's equally important to listen to our intuition because it ultimately benefits us. Neglecting to listen to our intuition carries consequences, as it leads to being overly pragmatic in our approach as self-leaders. We rely too heavily on our analytical mind and disregard the emotional connection. Leadership also involves emotions. There are moments when you simply feel that something didn't go well and sense a misalignment.

INTUITIVE LEADERSHIP

Working with your intuition allows you to have more and more levels of self alignment. It allows you to be more authentic. It gives you an opportunity to reflect a lot of truthfulness. I would like to go into the term of leadership intuition or intuitive leadership because it is a form of intelligence or instinct that we apply in leadership.

Intuitive leadership goes hand in hand with purposeful leadership. If you are following a purpose, you are driving towards something that has a value or a meaning, and you want to be somebody who is driving every interaction that you have with other people or every decision that you take leaning on your intuition. This means you are living a purposeful life.

INTUITIVE **LEADERSHIP** *goes hand in hand with* PURPOSEFUL **LEADERSHIP**

Leaning on intuition will also help you in that process. There are things in us that our gut feeling catches before our intellect does. Your instincts are always ready 24/7, and no matter how much we try to ignore them, they start to bug us in one way or another. As leaders, there is so much importance and emphasis on when we tap into our intuition.

In a messy situation, it is highly recommended that we do that. When there is a problem or a challenge that you don't have a lot of information about, if there is something that is requiring exchange or a shift in perspective when you are passing through a process of crisis and you need to rationalise things, but there is not much rationalization to be done, you need to take a quick decision.

This is where your intuition kicks in. When there is any situation that is not clear, we get more understanding by reflecting on it. Listening to all this insightful intuition inside of us, we are able to upgrade our leadership to a different level. One of the questions that could come up is, can intuitive leadership be taught? Absolutely it can be taught!

BECOMING INTUITIVE LEADERS

It is taught that we all have intuition inside of us; we just sometimes choose whether to align with it or not. The first crucial step in tapping into our intuition is to create some quiet time and be fully present during that time.

This involves disconnecting from everything around us, being still, and looking within ourselves. We can achieve this through practices like meditation or mindfulness breathing, or by engaging in activities that help us reflect on the present moment. It's about connecting with our values, allowing them to guide us, and carefully observing the situation.

Our purpose and values will always drive our intuition. When we feel that something aligns with our personal values, our intuition is at its best, playing its strongest role alongside us. Another way to cultivate intuitive leadership is to have clarity about our purpose or intention.

to cultivate **INTUITIVE LEADERSHIP** *have clarity about your* **PURPOSE** *or* **INTENTION**.

In the following chapters, we will gain a clearer understanding of our intention and purpose, which will provide us with deeper insights into intuition. While rationality is essential, we also recognise the value of these insights that arise from the wisdom of leadership we have collectively developed.

One the other things that is important when we are trying to develop our intuitive leadership is that we stay on the course of action and do not change. We need to trust and execute the choices of our decision. We do not go away from that decision.

We don't have to dwell on analysis paralysis but more on reflection and seeking to understand. When something doesn't feel right, what does our body tell us? Our body reflects a certain reaction. It could be like a fast heartbeat, it could be a feeling of breathlessness, or it could be that you're feeling excitement. It could be numbness or something that is showing up in your body. Looking at doing body scans on our body when something feels right or does not feel right is paying attention to all these physical cues that communicate to us about what is right or wrong for us.

GRATITUDE

Taking into consideration all the "Aha!" moments that we face, one of the things that helps a lot in developing intuition is leaning into gratitude. Gratitude has a very big role in pushing you towards intuition.

One of my favourite quotes is, "A grateful heart is a magnet for miracles." What do we mean by miracles? We don't mean miracles by magic, but miracles of being able to understand yourself more, to be able to take the right decision, live an aligned, purposeful, and helpful life. It is very essential that we lean in on gratitude because gratitude allows us to be aligned. And why gratitude? Because gratitude is a choice. An attitude of gratitude is developing the deliberate habit of expressing thanks on a regular basis for both significant and insignificant things.

DEVELOPING
INTUITION
is leaning into
GRATITUDE.

It is about you being grateful and thankful for whatever is happening around you at all times and looking at ways where you are able to see the positive in the situation. From a gratitude point of view, I'm not talking here about positive thinking, I am talking about grateful thinking.

I'm not undermining that you will be facing issues, but what is this trying to teach you? When you are facing the issues, what else are you grateful for? I strongly believe that a lot of emphasis needs to be put on gratitude.

Automatically your mind will be shifting towards gratitude rather than just problem finding or probably resentment. You become more responsive and confident and accurate in the way that you are analysing your emotions. You are in a flow. You are having a deeper sense of knowing because you are leaning on your gratitude.

you are having
A DEEPER SENSE OF
KNOWING

because
YOU ARE LEANING ON YOUR
GRATITUDE.

When you're leaning on your gratitude, you are trying to listen to your gut more because our nature is a grateful nature.

OUR
NATURE *is a*
GRATEFUL NATURE.

INTUITION IN BUSINESS

Throughout my career, I have decided to move different leaders within departments, although they may not have had the experience for the shift. I faced a lot of challenges in the past because it was just not the normal situation, or this is not the structured hierarchy of career growth. However, I believed inside myself that we would be able to develop these team members even from different areas and we would be able to move them from being specialists in their own roles to becoming generalist. This would also allow them to experience leadership growth. Something inside felt that it was right and I wanted to apply it.

After a lot of challenging conversations, I was able to tap into my intuition and convince my leadership team to accept these moves. This subtle voice that resided in me confirmed that I was taking the right path, and it has proven me right. Although it was such an underrated business decision, it showcased development in their leadership skills, communication skills, and in their ability to trust that they could face anything.

I encourage that when we give ourselves permission to see things the way they are and to strengthen them and to believe in what we think is right, this develops a lot of leadership intuition inside of us. Intuition is a skill.

Why do we call it intuition? Because it's not only an experience, but also a skill with an experience that we are applying. Learning from people's behaviours around us and getting to know the people for what they are, has been very helpful for me in strengthening my intuition and also challenging the status quo, allowing myself to see things from a different perspective because there is a vision inside. It maximised the value of my intuition, and it allowed me not to stereotype people's paths. I'm not saying we just have to act on intuition alone. We need to act on intuition and at the same time, we can also lean in on the facts that are around us.

ENEMIES OF INTUITION

Sometimes we do not like to face change as we feel challenged to shift the routine. However, let us dive in some of the enemies of intuition.

Intuition is sometimes mistaken for laziness, as it can make us reluctant to step out of our comfort zone. We might say, "No, this is my way, and it's the only way I want to do it because it's what I've always done." However, there's something inside of us telling us otherwise, yet we refuse to listen. This is one of the enemies of intuition.

Another enemy of intuition is failing to gather the proper perspective in any given situation. Before making a decision, it's important to consider the facts while also tuning into our intuitive nature to make an aligned decision. Looking at different perspectives and allowing ourselves to think and feel the right next step is the correct approach.

There must be a balance between trusting our feelings and considering the facts at hand. We should retain our current feelings while also being in tune with the surrounding facts.

Another challenge to intuition is when we assume we are aligned but deep down we're not. We align ourselves with someone else's values, whether it's a person or a company, even if they don't align with us. We may do this to feel a sense of belonging.

Creating space for our personal input and considering the facts around us is essential. When we are aligned, we can see things from different perspectives.

It's important to consistently check in with ourselves and incorporate daily practices like gratitude journaling or paying attention to emotional and physical cues. This is the only way we can grow and develop our intuition.

Reflecting on past situations where we followed our intuition, whether it served us or not, is also crucial for self-understanding.

By now, I hope you understand the power of intuition and how to utilise it. When used correctly, intuition can lead to a better understanding of our purpose and inspire action. Journaling can be a useful tool for reflecting on any situation we face.

CALL to █INTUITION█

For the next 30 days every day, keep a gratitude journal.

- Every morning, in your gratitude journal, write three things for which you are grateful.
- Every evening, write three things for which you are grateful from the day that has passed.

You will start to see the shift in your mindset and the shift in your ability to look for things with grateful eyes. This leads us to the next chapter where we will be talking about purpose.

CHAPTER 11

THE PURPOSEFUL POSSIBILITY

THE SECRET OF PASSION IS PURPOSE. A TRUE SENSE OF FULFILLMENT

R. Sharma (2011) in his book, *A Leadership Wisdom From The Monk Who Sold His Ferrari*, said, "When you know your why, the hows just start showing up."

Main factors of not finding our purpose, or help in finding our purpose are some of the details that we covered before, like limiting beliefs and self-judgment, getting in touch with our values and doing what we are passionate about with a beginner's mindset.

The SECRET OF PASSION *is* PURPOSE.

A TRUE SENSE OF FULFILLMENT.

Tuning into our being and balancing our doing and being also helps us to identify our purpose. Leaning on gratitude is something that guides us to get clarity on our purpose as well as an understanding that inside of us there is an inner power. Only then we can lean on our intuition. All of these are frameworks to help us drive towards understanding our purpose. I was told that having a purpose statement makes it easier for you to make decisions aligned to your values and helps you to stay motivated as you work towards your personal goals. This process requires self-reflection, finding where your passions lie, and feedback from people whose opinion we trust.

Tuning into our
BEING
and
balancing our
DOING & BEING
being helps us to identify our
PURPOSE.

By the end of this chapter, we will go through why you are seeking a purpose in life, and I will share my own journey into my own purpose and how I have come to that purpose that now provides a framework for the actions that I take in my life. This doesn't mean that I had to stop doing what I'm currently doing, but it opened the horizon to more fulfilling activities that speak to my soul.

Abraham Maslow once said, "If you plan on being anything else than you are capable of being, you will probably be unhappy all the days of your life." This is such a powerful statement, and we lose sense of contentment once we do not know what is filling our cup. We give so much emphasis to the material things, power, titles, and status as the source of fulfillment, but with all of that we might at times feel that there is something missing.

This goes back again to us identifying what the benefits are of being aware of our values, which we covered earlier. It is quite important for us to understand that having alignment with our values not only helps us look into a purposeful life, but also helps us to take actions towards a life of impact. It's optional, not required, to make your career the only reflection of your own identity. The secret of living a purposeful life is understanding that it is mainly a life of adventure and pleasure, and finding meaning in everything that we currently do. It makes a huge difference in the quality of our life because we feel more engaged. We feel that we are doing something that makes us feel connected, that gives a sense of care and support to everything that is around us, and we reap the benefits. We feel that our presence is giving a purpose to something bigger around us.

THE SECRET OF LIVING A
PURPOSEFUL LIFE
is finding
MEANING IN EVERYTHING THAT WE DO.

When we say purposeful life, it is living a life of purpose.

WHEN WE SAY
PURPOSEFUL
LIFE,
it is living
A LIFE OF
PURPOSE.

GROW YOUR SOUL AND CLEAN YOUR SOIL

A few years ago, I wrote an article on LinkedIn called, "Grow Your Soul and Clean Your Soil." This article went quite viral. Back then I didn't know where this need to write was coming from. It was confirming the fact that I am on a path, but this path was yet to become clear.

The article is as follows, "What is a good soil? We were taught that in order for anything to grow, it needs a good soil. What is a good soil? It is only the good soil that would help grow a healthy crop. A good soil can be created, and every experienced gardener knows the secret of building a great soil for a great garden."

"When the soil is ready and whether we are experienced planters or not, and even if we think we are not, we did plant some seeds. The care for them differs from watering habits to weather conditions and other factors. We learned this with experience and some of the instructions that are given to us, but when we start the schedule of how to water the plants, when we add fertilizers and we adjust it according to the needs of the plant, we wanted to grow and become greener and bigger. We adapt to the change and feel the sense of achievement when we see the plants growing. This is also a reflection that souls can also grow. Our souls can grow. They grow through the journey of life. Through this journey, we fill the thirst of our soul."

"Is this as simple as a growing plant? Given that we are all different. Do we need different soils? Each of us follows an individual path. We are different and that's the beauty of it. We are unique. We come to this life free as a baby, happy, simple, and enjoying every moment. Then we start growing and suddenly that excitement sometimes stops. We face challenges, we get hurt. We start embracing fear and we start hindering our abilities. And here we are, we allow the external factors to mess up with our free soul, and then our inner soil gets affected. It gets intoxicated, filled with various residues like anger, low self-esteem, sadness, and negative self-talk. We lose our connection with freedom and that emotional freedom that used to drive us before, which is the sky is the limit. You can do it."

"This becomes our wake-up call. We can grow our soul no matter what has happened, no matter what we have faced, no matter what we felt guilty about, no matter how we have acted, we can definitely grow our soul, and we are the gardeners of our soul and we can create the masterpiece of ourselves. You are the gardener of your soul. You can create the masterpiece of you. Take a step back and enjoy a deep breath. Do not underestimate what would five minutes of closed eyes in silence do to you. It shuts the mind, cutting down the thoughts, keeping you in complete relaxation, no rush, no pushing. You are only connected with the strong power in this universe. You're being brought to your own self-awareness. You can even take your soul for a walk. You go with your body and take your soul with you. Your soul then will realize the beauty of nature and anything that is beautiful."

"Improving your soil, removing those residues. It only starts by forgiving yourself and letting go. Do not let the past hold you. Is the past going to change your present? No, it won't. Accept it and let go of this past and whatever pains it has caused or still causing you, accept that it cannot change the present. Just tell yourself between parenthesis, 'Dear past, thank you for the lesson. It made me what I am today. I choose to let go and move on. I can and I will be kind to myself. I am stepping into the best version of myself.' While cleaning your own soul. Some of the steps you can do are the below. Practice the art of kindness. Yes, it is an art. What kind of vibes do you want to be surrounded with? Vibes of kindness is what your soul nurtures on. Practice kindness to yourself. First, take care of you. Your body requires food and exercise and so does your soul. It needs kindness and love. Change any negative self-talk into positive affirmations of kindness. Pay it forward. Help someone in need or do some volunteer work."

"There is nothing more self-fulfilling than creating a cycle of giving. You create it in the receiver too. It makes us connect to each other as human beings. We feel with another person. We give the receivers gifts and the cycle continues. It spreads gratefulness and appreciation. Fuel your passion. Passion is a big word which we need to dwell more into. Fuel that passion. Do more of what you like. Ask yourself, 'What am I passionate about?' By now you probably know the answer to this question. A better way of asking it. If I had to do what I like, what would I spend the day doing? The answer to this question is key. Remove the excuses of, 'I am too busy or I don't have time.' Make time for you. Put it in your calendar whether you want to learn how to dance or you want to learn how to cook a special dish. Find the time for it. And while you are in the process, befriend only who encourages you towards your passion."

"Use your vibe to attract your tribe. One line I personally enjoy hearing, 'Your vibe attracts your tribe.' Be around people who share the same passion and who are playing the role in pushing you forward. Research where and how you can work towards your passion. Giving time to your passion is a sign of self-love and nurturing of your soul. My personal advice is, between parenthesis, whatever inspires you, build on that inspiration. Do what your love to do and what fascinates your heart. Unleash your talent, be dedicated and experiment. Don't dwell into successes or failures. It's all a step forward. Reflect passion in the life of others and enjoy your creative journey."

Why am I sharing the article that I have written back then? Because this was more or less kind of the guiding principles of how I wanted to grow my soul and grow into living a purposeful life.

I have shared earlier about the authenticity crisis that I have faced before and how I wanted to get to know myself more and why I ended up doing what I'm currently doing. This just a reflection of how we can look into some of the factors or the tools that can help us elaborate more on our purpose.

ROAD TOWARDS PURPOSE

Knowing our values and getting clarity on our limiting beliefs are key in this journey. Spending time with people that inspire you and identify what brings you joy is also favourable. Reading about those who inspire you and being part of a community that reflects some of the things that you stand up for can help us discover our mission. Practicing self-acceptance and self-compassion as we covered in the previous chapters, taking time for yourself and practicing gratitude guides us in connecting the dots. Of course, we cannot forget the thing that I always speak about, unlearn and relearn. If there is something that hasn't been serving you, unlearn that from your actions, unlearn it from your behaviours, unlearn it from your memories and relearn new things that help you.

Studies have proven throughout the years that living a purposeful life has great side effects on us. Purpose strengthens our immune system. It has a health benefit, which is very impressive, because when we are living a purposeful life, we are protecting our brains by displaying so much of physical signs of cognitive degeneration. When we reflect this cognitive degeneration, this means there are neural pathways that are being created in our brains and they are re-routing, and they help us in living a healthier life. This is one of the great side effects of having a purpose in life.

Another thing is that it encourages longevity, because you are feeling that there is something that you look forward to because you're living a life of intention and hope. When you are identifying your intention, it helps you drive your purpose and also gives you clarity on your direction. Being purposeful also has a very strong emphasis on energy and willpower because you see some of the results coming up in your actions. Your time is being maximised. Your leisure time is being maximised. Your money is being maximised because you are putting your efforts into energy that is reflecting back to you. You have stronger connections for those around you because you are accepting them the way they are, and all your actions are going towards the positive relationship that you have with them.

PURPOSEFUL VISION STATEMENT

Living a purposeful life is a life worth living. One of the things that I always encourage people to develop is their own vision statement. The need to identify our own vision statement is key to help us align our personal values and our goals. It can be focused both on long-term dreams and professional goals. We can always lean on our vision statement. Words have a lot of power, and when we are committed to our vision, we can always lean on it when we are faced with adversity or the saboteurs that present themselves.

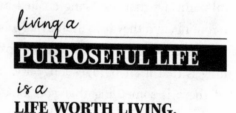

living a
PURPOSEFUL LIFE
is a
LIFE WORTH LIVING.

Identifying our own vision statement is writing down what is important for us and talking about it to people who we trust, and putting into motion those important goals that align with the vision statement that we currently have. In order for you to have a vision, it's very important to do some of the activities that we have shared in the previous chapters.

Here we are not talking about a company vision statement, we are talking about a personal vision statement for you. You are that specific brand that you are trying to be, the personal project of your future. Dream big and focus on your own success. Use the present tense, infuse it with passion and make it very, very inspiring. Align it with your values and with your goals and prepare to be committed to some time in order to put your vision and plan for communicating your vision.

Some of the people put their vision statement on Post-it notes, on their mirrors, in their car, in their offices, in areas where they see it.

I always like to share stories of people who have been impactful throughout my life, and they are some of the people who I might have read about or listened to their lectures or read their books.

(Dyer, 2015) has shared in one of his blogs in the past detailing that when he was a teacher, at some point, he wanted to go visit his father's grave and speak to him because of all the anger that he had towards him. When he went to his grave in Biloxi, Mississippi in 1974, he was quite upset with him because he felt his father had left them. When he was standing there, there was an inner-knowing and an inner voice that helped him. Previously, he had been very angry with his father, and now he was experiencing a moment of forgiveness that turned his whole life upside down. He speaks that this moment had changed everything. After that, he quit his job. He became a writer. He changed the way he saw his relationships. He stopped being angry and lost all the rage that he carried inside of him. That was the special moment of forgiveness that helped him to shift into a purposeful life, which he says specifically inspired him for a greater purpose.

In his blog, he says: "Inspiration comes from moving back in spirit and connecting to the seven faces of intention. When you feel inspired, what appear to be risky becomes a path you feel compelled to follow. The risks are gone because you are following your bliss, which is the truth within you. This is love working in harmony with your intention, especially if you do not feel love, you do not feel the truth." (*Inspiration and Purpose*, 2014)

This is why inspiration is such an important part of your intention to live a purposeful life. He dedicated his life to speak about an inspirational life. He has written many books and inspired many people, and he is somebody who has helped me in the path of looking at my own purpose.

We all know Oprah Winfrey and her successful story. We understand Oprah because of what she has become today, but what we don't know is that she never gave up and she continued on developing herself and trusting in herself. Oprah is currently known as a self-made woman who rose into what she is today. Oprah believes, "the best way to succeed is to discover what you love and then find a way to offer it to others in the form of service." She also says, "Passion is energy. Feel the power that comes from focusing on what excites you." (Cook, 2020)

Robin Sharma, a former lawyer, made the bold decision to quit his job and independently publish his first book at a Kinko's copy shop. Assisted by his mother as an editor, he printed 2000 copies and stored them in his kitchen. These copies were then distributed to his family, friends, and colleagues. His second book, "The Monk Who Sold His Ferrari," also began as a self-published work until he was discovered by Ed Carson, the former president of HarperCollins. Since then, he has been living his life purpose. (*Robin Sharma | Official Website of the #1 Bestselling Author*, n.d.)

INSPIRATION

is an

IMPORTANT
PART OF YOUR
INTENTION

to live a

PURPOSEFUL
LIFE.

Now let me share my own story. As I mentioned before, I had an authenticity crisis regarding who I am without my work title. I believe there's a lot I can contribute to the world.

I felt quite down because of this and I wanted to understand the origin of these thoughts and the articles I was writing. I embarked on a journey with my coach to explore these limiting beliefs, my values, and what I truly want to do and why. As we progress, you will gain insight into my personal purpose.

Allow me to share my personal purpose, which reflects the world I aspire to live in and inspire others to create: "I want to live in a world where people live their lives to their extreme potential, guided by their abilities, mastering their strengths, and achieving their dreams one step at a time."

For this to work for you, you need to stop seeking external validation. When you develop your core values and embrace a life driven by growth, your purpose will evolve, and you will live in alignment with it. Reflect on the factors and requirements that help you stay aligned with your purpose. I want to emphasise the importance of living a purposeful life.

YOU NEED TO
STOP SEEKING
EXTERNAL VALIDATION.

Carroll (2009) in "Alice in Wonderland," says "If you do not know where you are going, any road will get you there."

Having clarity about your purpose will now lead us to discuss how we lead our lives.

When you
DEVELOP YOUR CORE VALUES,
EMBRACE A LIFE DRIVEN BY GROWTH,

YOUR PURPOSE WILL EVOLVE, *and*
YOU WILL LIVE IN ALIGNMENT WITH IT.

CALL *to* PURPOSE

- Relist your set of values as prepared in the previous activities.
- Write down your interest and some of your skills. In what activities do you feel energised?
- In your personal and professional life, list all of your successes, how they make you feel, and what you are most proud of.
- You are prepared to write your own vision statement once you have thoroughly written responses to the above. When writing your vision statement, start with a list of keywords inspired by the above.
- Write your statement in the first person and express your aspirations for the future. The remarks should be written as though you are currently bringing them about in your life.

Now that we have identified our purpose, we will get into self-leadership.

CHAPTER 12

POWER OR EMPOWER

THE REAL POWER OF LEADERSHIP IS TO EMPOWER

How can leadership be linked mainly to power when leadership has less to do with authority and more to do with mindset? Many people have related leadership to power.

Five different types of power were found in 1959 research by two social psychologists, John R. P. French and Bertram Raven. They categorised it into formal power and personal power. Formal power is the coercive power, the reward power, the legitimate power. Personal power is the expert power or the referent power.

THE REAL POWER *of*
LEADERSHIP
is to
EMPOWER

In addition to the above, we have covered that leadership is meant to be intuitive. It is meant to be authentic and empowering. The deepest score of true leadership is through empowerment, and empowerment starts with you before it moves with others. You are empowered. You have to look into yourself and give this to yourself, self-empowerment.

YOU ARE EMPOWERED!

give this to yourself:
SELF-EMPOWERMENT

(Manz, 1983) A proponent of self-leadership said, "All human beings are self-leaders. However, not all self-leaders are effective at self-leading." Such a powerful statement that self-leading is not something that every leader has, but it is supposed to be the core of how we lead our lives. Everyone has one or more than one person that they are inspired by. They like their lifestyle, the way that they carry themselves; probably, if at work, the way they manage and lead their teams. We get inspired by the way that they are leading their life.

By the end of this chapter, you will learn how we can shift into self-empowerment in the way that we lead ourselves in order for us to lead others. You don't need a title to be a leader. In reality, you are first a leader of your own life before you became a leader in anything in your life such as leading a team or being in charge of a group or in charge of your family. Hence, better decisions are made and stronger relationships are built when leaders are tuned into their self-empowerment.

YOU DON'T NEED
A TITLE
to be
A LEADER.

Do you remember your favourite teacher? I do. What were the qualities that they displayed? I recall one of my favourite teachers in school. When I was at high school, I recall being impacted by my English teacher. I loved studying English Literature, but the reason was more to do with how she led this class. She was very distinctive and more modern in her style. She was straight forward, outgoing, fun, motivating, and above all had a high level of integrity. She would communicate a shared purpose and vision for us and our futures which made us always reflect and dream. She would listen to us and advise us on anything that we needed guidance in. Without undermining all other teachers who I have encountered, she was a true reflection of a leader. And there it was, my first connection to leadership, through her. She represented somebody who was fully in charge of their own belief system and their life, a true reflection of the leader.

Here through this teacher was my first connection to leadership. Fast forward to the amazing leaders I've had throughout the years. They had qualities of a true leader from listening skills, being empathetic, fun, leading by example, engaging, motivating, agile and adaptable. They also had a lot of impact and influence.

What is common amongst all is that they have a growth mindset and a high level of self-awareness.

We have covered already the self-awareness part by having identified our values and intentions on why we do what we do. This had made us understand what drives our behaviour and how transformation can happen once we understand ourselves more.

We have discussed the importance of passion in our lives and how it motivates us. We have done that through the compassion towards the self. We have identified how limiting beliefs play an important role in our lives. We've also covered getting clarity on our core purpose.

Now the most important question is: "Are my daily actions aligned with my values and are these actions helping me progress towards my core purpose?" This is the foundation of expressing all your skills, knowledge, passion, values and capability.

SELF-LEADERSHIP

Why is self-leadership important? It has been proven that self-leadership can cause you an increased level of efficiency and an elevated level of productivity because you know what you want, and you are working towards it. It reflects a lower reaction to stress and a higher motivation and accountability. It helps you have stronger relationships with family members or co-workers, gives you a better mindset for success and reflects you as an inspiration for others.

An example of one of my leaders who inspired me at work was a leader in Dubai who moved there with his family. His name was Ian. He possessed a high level of awareness and understood the capabilities of the team around him. He knew his strengths and how to influence others to be the best at what they do. The work environment was highly engaging, allowing everyone to show up as themselves without being overly structured or restricted from innovation. Being aware and having a high level of emotional intelligence supported us in becoming a strong team and achieving great results, both personally and professionally. He was one of my favourite leaders.

Now, let's delve into the definition of self-leadership. It is the ability to lead yourself in order to achieve your personal and professional goals. Through self-leadership, you gain understanding of who you are, what you can achieve, where you want to go, and how to manage your emotions and behaviours.

GOALS AND MINDSET

What about our goals? There are two types of goals: outcome goals and process goals. An example of an outcome goal would be as follows. Let's say you want to be a fit person by the end of this month, or you want to be able to, for example, speak a certain language in three months. The process goal would be to register into the class, show up to the class, practice in the class. This is the difference between these two types of goals.

Clarity on our goals and what we want will help us create the road map for the way forward.

Once you identify your purpose, it is important to ensure that all actions are aligned with this purpose and why are they aligned with this purpose. Taking value-based decisions from a high energy level and not from a low energy level.

Why is it important to take value-based decisions from a high energy level? Because if we are at a very low energy level, we are going to be looking from a victim mindset and not from a winner's mindset. We will be not leaning on our values that we've explained before. It is very important to be at the right mindset, truly aligned with our values when we're trying to make a decision that is very important for us.

EMOTIONAL AWARENESS

Practicing emotional awareness is key in self-leadership. Emotional awareness means knowing when feelings are present in ourselves and others.

It will be easier for you to communicate effectively with others if you have emotional awareness, or the capacity to comprehend emotions. You will communicate more clearly if you are emotionally aware. You'll become aware of other people's emotions and how their state of mind affects how they communicate.

We need to ask ourselves: "What is the emotion that I am feeling and why? And how can it relate to my values, and why is it triggering me?"

Once we have a recognition of these questions, we will be digging deeper into reasons why these things are triggering us at the moment and how can we make a shift because now we have clarity.

In challenging situations, it is important to be having a perspective. When you have a perspective, you are looking at the challenging situation from an eagle's eye, not necessarily putting yourself in the situation. This doesn't undermine that you need to feel the emotions of hurt or probably shame or probably disappointment or anything that might have triggered you in that challenging situation. However, at the same time, having a perspective about it will also drive a high level of self-awareness inside us.

Developing an emotional intelligence through more emotional awareness helps us to grow our self-management and self-awareness. You are aware of how your own emotions impact your ideas and actions. You are confident in yourself and are aware of your talents and areas of development. This can develop you to be more socially aware too. You will develop the ability to create and sustain positive connections, speak clearly, motivate and influence people, collaborate well with others, and handle disagreement.

developing our
EMOTIONAL
INTELLIGENCE
through more
EMOTIONAL
AWARENESS

HELPS US TO GROW
our
SELF-MANAGEMENT
and
SELF-AWARENESS

MINDFULNESS AND REFLECTION

Practicing mindfulness and reflection are two very high recommendations in trying to dig into self-awareness inside us. When we are having a silent moment, this is when the thoughts start to come, and this is when we can reflect back on what we are thinking or what we are feeling or allow ourselves to be aligned to the present moment and what is showing up.

Listening to your intuition and reflecting internally as we have covered that in the previous chapters will give us a lot of insight.

FEEDBACK

Seeking feedback from a trusted source with the intention to grow is also key in self-awareness. This reflects growth mindset. I say trusted source because it is important to get feedback from those who believe in you and want the best for you. You do not need to accept feedback from those who feel that they have been nominated to give their opinion about your life.

COMMITMENT OVER CONVENIENCE

The last thing I would recommend is to choose commitment over convenience and have a high level of self-discipline when it comes to certain actions that we have put in place. It is sometimes our outcome, or our goals might be challenging, but when we harness these challenging goals or outcomes for us, we are stretching ourselves, thereby giving ourselves a commitment and a promise that we want to achieve what we want. Then accordingly, all the actions that we are putting together need to reflect this.

The psychologist Goleman (2005) points out in his bestseller *Emotional Intelligence,* "Exceptional leaders distinguish themselves because of superior self-leadership."

SELF-LEADERSHIP QUALITIES

What are the qualities of self-leadership? Self-leadership has qualities of self-honesty, self-drive, integrity, compassion, self-discipline, curiosity, accountability, courage, humility, willingness, assertiveness and inner faith. Do these values ring a bell for you when you do your values exercise? I am sure there must be few of those that are in your top ten values list.

Cultivating self-leadership helps us to master our behaviour and gives us an opportunity to lead our lives to our highest potential. Self-leadership isn't very common, so it is helpful to look at some role models that have displayed self-leadership around us.

As I mentioned earlier, having the qualities of self-leadership is quite key. If we dig into some of them, self-leadership is about a high level of self-awareness. With self-awareness we can observe a situation that triggers us and then identify why we have some rigid blocks against some ideas and we are able to get more clarity about it.

I've spoken about self-regulation. It is our ability to regulate and be open to change and be comfortable with any ambiguity that could come across our way. Being empathetic is key because we are showing that this quality requires a connection to another person's feelings, and then it will help us to treat everything and according to our reactions, emotional reactions to it. These are quite key in displaying self-leadership.

R. Sharma (2010) once said, "Work offers you a daily platform to discover the leader within. It is a chance every day to reclaim more of the potential you have buried and awaken the dormant relationship between the current you and your absolute best. It is an opportunity to express more of your latent creativity and a whole lot more of your precious humanity."

As I mentioned, self-leadership isn't common. Why is that? Self-leadership is rare because many of us do not want to go into any psychological development or any development at all because we are afraid of what we might find. We are also afraid of who we would become if we tackled some of the development that we require in order for us to go into this level of self-awareness.

Self-leadership does not happen by accident. It takes daily practice. It needs attention, takes a lot of progress and reflection as well as emotional intelligence. With emotional intelligence, self-regulation, self-awareness, motivation, empathy and social skill, as Goleman (2005) characterises it, it may be uncomfortable to other people when they are looking into all this and wanting to grow into a positive wellbeing state.

There is fear in this process, and sometimes we do not want to go out of our comfort zone because we just want to be in our comfortable state. But I remind you, you are born to be great, so why don't you step into your greatness?

For you to step into your greatness and self-leadership, all previous work needs to be completed. Work on your values, tackle the limiting beliefs part, identify your strength, practice mindfulness, give time to self-reflection and identify your core purpose. Everything that we have covered in the chapters before is core work to lead us to self-leadership. We have been tackling drop by drop, step by step, the expansion of yourself. And here we are at the end of this chapter, and I would like to conclude it in few words.

WORK ON
KNOWING YOUR VALUES,

TACKLE YOUR
LIMITING BELIEFS,

IDENTIFY YOUR
STRENGTHS,

PRACTICE
MINDFULNESS,

GIVE TIME TO
SELF-REFLECTION,

and

IDENTIFY YOUR
CORE PURPOSE.

Self-leadership is ongoing and a never-ending platform on how you show up every day as yourself and as inspiration to others. Self-leadership is linked to self-growth. The more we grow and learn, the more we are able to know ourselves. The more we experience, the clearer it is for us how to react, understand why we feel what we are feeling, and what areas need more focus for us to realign.

SELF-LEADERSHIP

is linked to

SELF-GROWTH.

Do you believe that you are more than your title? Do you now believe that you are the human behind the title? You are re-leading your life.

Sinek (2011) in his book *Start With Why* said "Leadership is not about being in charge. Leadership is about taking care of those in your charge."

Today is the first day of the remainder of your life.

If someone asks you, "Who do you think you are," you should answer, "Whoever I want to be and I choose to be me."

IF SOMEONE ASKS YOU:

"Who do you think you are?"

YOU SHOULD ANSWER,

"Whoever I want to be and I choose to be me."

A quote that always inspires me from Alice in Wonderland is, "I cannot go back to yesterday because I was a different person then." (Carroll, 2009). Don't we all have this Alice in Wonderland moment?

To get over anything in your life, stop telling the story of your past and start creating the story of your future. Define the future vision of yourself. Observe your thoughts and actions as you go through your days. Remember that how you think and how you feel influences everything in your life. The moment you start feeling grateful and start to change all your negative emotions to hope and inspiration, you are already on the transformational path towards your dream life.

In this world, we might encounter mediocrity and many people in distraction mode. Some people do not focus. They do not pay attention to anything that is causing changes in their lives, and they don't pay attention to what are the needle movers of their goals.

It is your personal choice to be different, to grow and develop, to move from victimization to leadership and play the sports of heroism. Commitment to our goals, consistency in our actions and showing up no matter what, being self-aware, developing a skill, learning from our mistakes, curiously exploring new ideas, reflecting, putting plans and the lists goes on and on; these are the actions of heroism.

Each one of us has the potential of greatness and unlimited abilities. Whether your dream is too big or too small, everyone starts somewhere. They face scarcity, fear, uncertainty, but they don't allow these emotions to stop them and redirect them. They showed up for their dreams.

Commitment to self-discovery and a serious set of actions together with an open mindset will awaken the best version of yourself. Great opportunities are astonishingly disguised as impossible situations. With self-awareness and perspective shifting, we evolve, we learn, and we grow.

Through self-awareness, you can make better choices, and with these choices you are able to get, of course, new results and even great results. One day we wake up different, we have an authenticity crisis that says: "Welcome Home. Welcome home to alignment of your mind, body, and soul. Welcome home to the hero in you."

My personal purpose is that "I Want To Live In A World Where People Live Their Lives To Their Extreme Potential, Guided By Their Abilities, Mastering Their Strengths, And Achieving Their Dreams One Step At A Time."

> *I want to live in a world*
>
> Where People Live Their Lives
> To Their Extreme Potential,
> Guided By Their Abilities,
> Mastering Their Strengths,
> and Achieving Their Dreams
>
> One Step At A Time.

I am committed to enable transformation in people by inspiring them and helping them to be the aspiring leaders they can be, and to lead their lives with emotion, gratitude, and self-awareness.

This book is dedicated to my purpose. Maya Angelou once said, "By telling your story, you create a legacy that will resonate through generations." I hope that the stories you have heard in this book inspire you to create your own story.

CONCLUSION

Are you leading your life with a loud ego or a grounded presence? Leadership is all about authenticity. Self-leadership is the core of it all. Being true to yourself and your values is a reflection of trust and authenticity. This is where our personal purpose comes into play. Leaders need to be conscious of how their behaviours impact those they lead, and this initially includes themselves first. This is where self-awareness comes into play. A big ego can maybe create huge achievements, but it can result in huge destruction too. An unchecked ego can impact our perspective or misalign our values. It narrows our field of vision. An inflated loud ego can impact our behaviour, our decision making and our ability to learn more from what is happening around us.

Leading with grounded presence requires selflessness, reflection and above all courage.

It is leading with your authentic values. It is demonstrating through your actions that you practice the same values and behaviours you expect from those around you. It means you cultivate a grounded level of self-awareness. You are purposeful and committed. It is building trust based on ethical human values.

Grounded leaders are trustworthy leaders who demonstrate their integrity by always doing the right thing as it is in line with their values.

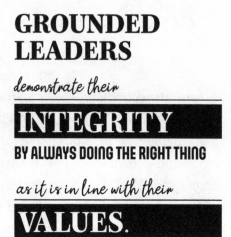

Discovering your purpose is the first step of living a meaningful and intentional life. Living your purpose is the utmost level of living the central motivating aims of your life—the reasons you get up in the morning.

LIVING YOUR
PURPOSE
is

THE UTMOST LEVEL OF LIVING THE CENTRAL MOTIVATING AIMS OF YOUR LIFE

THE REASONS

you get up in the morning.

Purpose can guide life decisions, influence behaviour, shape goals, offer a sense of direction, and create meaning.

We are all born with an inner guidance that tells us when we are on or off course by the amount of joy we are experiencing. Once we identify our purpose, we become aware of what we want and what we don't want. Clarity!

ONCE WE IDENTIFY OUR
PURPOSE,

we become aware of

WHAT WE WANT,

and

WHAT WE DON'T WANT.

CLARITY!

It is about aligning our goals with our life purpose and passion. Through the self-awareness journey, the goals get clearer and with clarity we become more fulfilled. Through goal setting, affirmations and visualisation, we start experiencing an intention. The goals and the intention are then supported by a set of actions and behaviours portraying our purpose. We start seeking new opportunities, new ideas and we experience a shift in mindset. I believe with the right tools, you can cultivate a mindset of purpose, and up-level every single aspect of your life, both personal and professional.

If you live by your values and listen to your heart, it becomes effortless. You are creating a mission and vision that others can follow.

What are the steps you are taking right now to be living and leading with your heart? Decide what's important to you. Reflect on desired direction in areas like relationships, family, friends, community, careers, parenting, art, sports, knowledge, hobbies, and many others.

Leading a purposeful life is part of leading a balanced life.

LEADING
A PURPOSEFUL LIFE

is part of

LEADING
A BALANCED LIFE.

Leading with your heart creates a story of connectedness, influence and empowerment.

LEADING WITH
YOUR HEART
creates a story of
CONNECTEDNESS,
INFLUENCE *and*
EMPOWERMENT.

You can build stronger sustainable teams when authenticity is the core of it all.

You will be fulfilled and content just by simply being "Purposely aligned with your purpose."

SIMPLY BE:
"Purposely aligned with your purpose."

you are

NOT YOUR TITLE.

you are

THE PERSON BEHIND THE TITLE.

REFERENCES

A quote by Miriam Adeney. (n.d.). https://www.goodreads.com/quotes/884213-you-will-never-be-completely-at-home-again-because-part

About Louise Hay | Bio & Timeline of Achievements. (2022, June 28). Louise Hay. https://www.louisehay.com/about/.

Cameron, J. M. (2002). *The Artist's Way: a spiritual path to higher creativity.* https://ci.nii.ac.jp/ncid/BB28969730

Carroll, L. (2009). *Alice in Wonderland*. The Floating Press.

Cook, J. (2020, September 9). 5 Things Every Entrepreneur Can Learn From Oprah. *Forbes.* https://www.forbes.com/sites/jodiecook/2020/09/09/5-things-every-entrepreneur-can-learn-from-oprah/?sh=4e360d101f7d.

Deepak Chopra™. (2022, December 27). *About - Deepak Chopra™.* https://www.deepakchopra.com/about/.

Dispenza, J. (2013). *Breaking The Habit of Being Yourself: How to Lose Your Mind and Create a New One.* Hay House, Inc.

Dweck, C. S. (2007). *Mindset: The New Psychology of Success.* National Geographic Books.

Dyer, W. W. (2004). *The Power of Intention: Change the Way You Look at Things and the Things You Look at Will Change.* Hay House, Inc.

Dyer, W. W. (2007). *Change Your Thoughts, Change Your Life: Living the Wisdom of the Tao.* Hay House, Inc.

Dyer, W. W. (2009). *Your Erroneous Zones: Escape Negative Thinking and Take Control of Your Life.* Piatkus Books.

Dyer, W. W. (2015, September 16). *My Greatest Teacher.* Dr. Wayne W. Dyer. https://www.drwaynedyer.com/blog/my-greatest-teacher/.

Ericsson, A., & Pool, R. (2017). *Peak: Secrets from the New Science of Expertise.* HarperOne.

Gallup, Inc. (2023). State of the Global Workplace Report - Gallup. In *Gallup.com.* https://www.gallup.com/workplace/349484/state-of-the-global-workplace-2022-report.aspx.

Gardner, C. (Producer), & Muccino, G. (Director). (2006). The Pursuit of Happyness [Motion picture]. United States: Columbia Pictures.

Gilbert, E. (2007). *Eat, Pray, Love: One Woman's Search for Everything.* A&C Black.

Goleman, D. (2005). *Emotional Intelligence: Why It Can Matter More Than IQ.* Bantam.

Hay, L. (1995). *You Can Heal Your Life.* Hay House, Inc.

Inspiration and Purpose. (2014, September 19). Dr. Wayne W. Dyer. https://www.drwaynedyer.com/press/inspiration-purpose/.

Robin Sharma | Official Website of the #1 Bestselling Author. (n.d.). https://www.robinsharma.com/about-robin.

Sharma, R. (2010). *The Leader Who Had No Title: A Modern Fable on Real Success in Business and in Life.* Simon and Schuster.

Sharma, R. (2011). *Leadership Wisdom From The Monk Who Sold His Ferrari: The 8 Rituals of Visionary Leaders.* HarperCollins Canada.

Sharma, R. (2018). *The 5AM Club: Own Your Morning. Elevate Your Life*. HarperCollins.

Sinek, S. (2011). *Start With Why: The Inspiring Million-Copy Bestseller That Will Help You Find Your Purpose*. Penguin UK.

Sparacino, B. (2018). *The Strength in Our Scars*.

Stanford University. (2021, September 16). *Your powerful, changeable mindset - Stanford Report*. Stanford Report. https://news.stanford.edu/report/2021/09/15/mindsets-clearing-lens-life/.

Street, F. (2021). Carol Dweck: A Summary of Growth and Fixed Mindsets. *Farnam Street*. https://fs.blog/carol-dweck-mindset/.

Tolle, E. (2008). *A New Earth: Awakening to Your Life's Purpose*. Christian Large Print.

Trent Slaney. (2013, April 11). *George Bernard Shaw quotes on reputation*. Ireland Calling. https://ireland-calling.com/george-bernard-shaw-quotes-reputation/.

AUTHOR BIO

Soumana is a Senior Hospitality Executive and a Leadership Strength Coach bringing in a wealth of experience. Soumana's outgoing personality and authentic approach towards leadership has made her content and input on self-awareness and personal leadership go viral attracting an engaged audience through her conversations on different channels.

Soumana is an advocate of people development and coaching, facilitating transformation by helping aspiring leaders in their development journey. She applies a strengths-based approach creating engagement and transformational change.

She is a supporter for diversity in leadership advising that in this modern and with the right combination of charisma, enthusiasm, self-assurance and skills, leadership goes beyond gender, race, ethnicity and religion and includes diversity of thought.

She believes that when given the right platform, people who think in different ways boost innovation, creativity, and problem solving. This combined with unique experiences and perceptions help strengthen productivity.

She always believed in equal opportunities that empowers individuals to be the best they can be and form a family of like-minded passionate people in any area of their life.

Soumana's personal purpose to live in a world where people live their lives to their extreme potential guided by their abilities, mastering their strengths and achieving their dreams one step at a time.

Soumana loves travelling, trying different cuisines along with art and photography as well as anything that can impact the wellbeing and all its elements.

EXTRAS

Soumana's outgoing personality and authentic approach towards leadership has made her content and input on self-awareness and personal leadership go viral attracting an engaged audience through her conversations on different channels.

Being a coach and a key note speaker, Soumana is active about personal development on various platforms and in diverse events.

Being strong believer in living a balanced and authentic life with a growth mindset and a passion for continuous learning, Soumana is a on a mission to bring her purpose to life and enable transformation in people by inspiring them to embrace their highest potential leaning on their own strengths.

She can be contacted on her website www.soumanaammar.com or on her Linked in account https://www.linkedin.com/in/soumanaammar.

NOTES